YOU

The Person

You

Want to Be

Also by Ruth Fedder: A GIRL GROWS UP

YOU
the person
you want to be

by RUTH FEDDER

Illustrated by Algot Stenbery

Whittlesey House

McGRAW-HILL BOOK COMPANY, INC.

New York   Toronto   London

THE FOLLOWING PERSONS have read the manuscript and given the author helpful advice during the preparation of this book: Professor Esther McD. Lloyd-Jones of Teachers College, Columbia University; Professor Kathern McKinnon of Hunter College, New York City; Dr. Bruce Robinson, former Director of the Department of Child Guidance of the Board of Education, Newark, New Jersey; and Dr. Albert J. Kaplan, Psychiatrist, Philadelphia, Pennsylvania, and Consulting Psychiatrist, Bucks County Public Schools.

The author acknowledges her debt to the writings of Henry Stack Sullivan, Erich Fromm, Rollo May, and Arthur Jersild. The inspiration and ideas which she has absorbed from them have become part of this book.

The author is grateful to her secretary, Mrs. Mabel Lampert, who has patiently typed and retyped the manuscript, and to her sister, Helma Fedder, who has continuously assisted in editing and proofreading.

SECOND PRINTING

Library of Congress Catalog Card Number: 57-12579

Published by Whittlesey House
A division of the McGraw-Hill Book Company, Inc.

Contents

Are You Someone You Like?

"I'M GETTING up—right now," Dick shouted in answer to his mother's call. He glanced guiltily at his watch. Not too bad. Then he remembered—he wasn't going to school to-day, so the insistent calling must be for a family conference on their problem child before Father left for the office.

He pulled on a bathrobe—then changed his mind. His father was neurotic about bathrobes at breakfast; it would be smart to get into slacks and shirt. This would not be an easy session.

To tell the truth, Father had been very decent last night —in a way that made it harder, more embarrassing. The heavy parent Dick could put up with, but who could cope with a confused and hurt parent?

So he had been suspended from school for a week. And for what?—talking. Did that make him a juvenile delinquent? Dear sister Diane was never suspended; she was a real prizewinner, that gal, right from kindergarten to college scholarship.

Wait a minute, though, that wasn't fair. Dick admitted that Diane never made a big deal about her prizewinning. Just the same, it was tough to have a smart sister who was "such a hard worker" that she'd even made the front page of the local newspaper last June for nailing down the biggest scholarship "any local high school student has ever been awarded"—he remembered the exact words! He'd been proud—in a way. But he had to live with that this year. Then the doctor kept him off the team because he'd had rheumatic fever years ago. And now this business! Everything happened to him—he even had to be the smallest guy in his class and listen to the girls call him "squirt." His fists doubled and he beat them on the bed.

He thought of last night. He felt ashamed. He had *wanted* to talk things over with his parents. Why hadn't he done it? His father had listened as Dick explained heatedly that all he'd done was, in a vocations class discussing "Does Your High School Record Count?" to shout out, "Well, I'm in school to have a good time. I'm not going to college and I don't care whether I work in school or not." For that, he'd been sent to the office and to detention hall. When he didn't show up in detention, the principal caught up with him the next day and told him he was suspended and he must bring his parents to school to talk over the matter.

Father hadn't bawled him out. Dick would have known how to handle that. Instead, Dick had become more and more embarrassed because his father kept saying confusedly, "I don't see why you did it."

Suddenly, Dick had burst out bitterly,

"'Course you don't see! How could you? How do you know what it's like to be sixteen and a 'squirt'!" Then Dick had rushed out of the room and, except for a grudging "goodnight" to his parents through his locked door, had talked to no one for the rest of the evening.

Why had he acted like that? His parents seemed to be trying to understand even when Dick admitted that he was "always talking out" in class, that the principal had warned him before and had sent letters home. His father had begun to talk about his passing up life's opportunities. Then his mother had interrupted, "But, Dick, why did you say you weren't going to college? You could if you wanted to— just as Diane did."

Maybe he was yellow. He'd just plain *refused* to talk.— But what good would it do? Gee, they couldn't make him grow a few inches or change the doctor's mind about his getting off the team. But why couldn't they let him be himself? Why did he always have to hear about his sister?

Anyhow, what did they expect him to do about himself? It was easy for grownups to talk. They could control things. They had the upper hand. Nothing ever got in their way. "I'll bet," Dick told himself, "if something did, they could hardly believe it. They'd probably just keep saying, 'This can't happen to me.'"

Or would they? Suddenly Dick sat bolt upright. He heard, for the first time, what his father had said last night, "Life's not soft for anybody, fellow! Neither the school nor the world owes you anything. It just gives you opportunities—you can make something of them if you will—if you stand up to things. Stop whining and excusing yourself for what you aren't—or haven't got. It's *your* life! When are you going to begin making the most of it?"

Last night, Dick thought solely in terms of "everything happens to me." He hated the world and himself. This morning, Dick is beginning to understand that people around him aren't just singling *him* out to "pick on" him. That's life—and he's part of it.

Dick is beginning to see that *he can do something* about what happens to him. Dick is beginning to recognize himself as a person—not a child to be buffeted around by his behavior—but a unique individual with ideas, abilities, and ambitions distinctly his own who can *choose* to respond in one of several different ways to every situation. He wants hard things to do to prove his courage. He is eager to "measure up" with other people; he is confident that everyone will recognize the new self as a person to be reckoned with! This estimate is important because Dick's hopes and fears about himself are largely a reflection of what he thinks others think about him. If Dick can get other people to consider him a likable, dependable person, he will inevitably so "rate" himself.

But each teenager is more than one person. Thus, another part of Dick asks, "*Can* I make myself over?" Engrossed in

10

past discouragements and shortcomings, this part of Dick is afraid to be different. What if people do not understand the new self or prize it as Dick does? They may "smack him down"—or make fun of him. Sometimes this scared self takes over.

The brave Dick planned to go down to breakfast and say something like, "Dad, you're looking at a guy who's been thinking about things. I'll go to school with you today and tell them that I believe I can cut out the foolishness and get to work. You said last night that it was my life and I should take over. I'm gonna start!"

Then, when Dick got downstairs, his mother told him that his father had been called to his office, and that the school interview had been postponed until afternoon. She added, anxiously, "Dick, your father and I are so worried about you. We want to help you. You know, if we didn't have you, we'd be alone now."

"Well, you've got me, and I guess you're stuck with me." Dick reached for his milk. He couldn't talk; something about her tone made him think he was a baby again. The old resentment took over; the new brave self retreated.

His mother looked at him helplessly. Then, abruptly, she rose, saying, "I'm going to the kitchen to make more coffee. I'll have a cup with you while you finish your breakfast."

Suddenly Dick hated himself for hurting his mother. "What a dope I am! Why couldn't I tell her what I planned to say—the speech I had all ready for Dad? What threw me?"

You know what threw him. The fearful part of him said, "She thinks you're a baby. She won't believe in your new self." Maybe Dick's mother did consider him a baby—and maybe she didn't. Dick was so afraid that she wouldn't recognize his new self that he gave her no chance to do so. As Dick realized what happened, he *determined* to try out the new self. "When she comes back, I'll keep that one part of me from scaring the new guy I found this morning."

Dick's mother was walking to the front door. He heard the click of the mailbox lid. She came back into the dining room opening a letter. "From Diane," she said, as she began to read. Dick winced. But his mother was smiling. "Poor kid! I'm so glad for her. Listen to this: 'My biggest moment in college, Mom! My new roommate is an inch taller than I am, so we can have our troubles together!' "

Dick looked blank. "What's that mean?"

"Oh, Dick!" His mother sounded almost reproachful. "You must know that Diane's height has always bothered her. After all, five feet ten inches is awfully tall for a girl. It's hard for her to find tall boys she likes. She went without dates lots of times last year because she was embarrassed about going out with *little* boys. But maybe you were too wrapped up in your own troubles to notice hers." She reached over and patted Dick's shoulder.

He stared. "You mean—Diane has troubles?"

His mother picked up her coffee cup as she looked back at him and began slowly. "Yes, Dick, like you—and me— and Dad. Your father wanted to have breakfast with us this morning, but one of the subcontractors called. He just had to go to the office. Things are going wrong in that home development again. Your father's worried because he's already had to pour into it some of the money he was saving for your college. But he's been more worried because you've seemed to resent even talking about college. . . ."

Dick interrupted, "You mean, Dad's saving money—for me—for college—with Diane's to pay too? You mean, you want me to go? Maybe I can get a job—or help Dad. . . ."

"Dick, that's fine," his mother smiled. "But your job now. . . ."

". . . is school." Dick finished her sentence. "I know, Mom. I think I can manage.—You know, Mom, you never told me before that everybody has troubles. I'm part of this family. I ought to know. . . ."

"You're right, Dick." His mother looked searchingly at him. "Maybe we've shielded you—we haven't realized how fast you were growing up. . . ."

"Well, I guess I *was* only a kid—until this morning." The words began to pour out. "Mom, will Dad be home for lunch before our appointment at school? I want to tell him I'll try to stop whining and excusing myself. I guess nobody's laying for me except me. I think I see the light. Anyhow, if everybody else in this house can do a job, I guess it's about time I pitch in. You're looking at a guy who'll go to school with Dad and take his medicine. You can count on me. You don't need to come along—Dad and I can manage."

Dick jumped up suddenly and clapped his mother on the back. "Let's go do the dishes. Guess I'll write a note to Sis then. Anyhow, her birthday's next week.—Oh yeah, Mom—tell Dad there'll be less aspirin needed around here in the future!"

"Aspirin?" his mother asked.

"Yes—you know, for headaches." But Dick didn't mean it as a joke.

It's Normal!

Would you say that now Dick will "live happily ever after"? If you mean that, from today on, Dick will have a life without problems—the answer is emphatically "no." How dull life would be! However, if you mean that because Dick is learning to understand himself and to face his problems, he will be equipped to live more happily, the answer is "yes." Life presents new problems every day; but Dick will meet them confidently because he is getting to work on the most important subject he—or you—has to learn in school or in life: self-knowledge.

Knowing yourself results from something quite different from taking required courses or accurate lecture notes, from writing term papers or passing examinations. Book knowledge—of psychology, particularly—can become just an academic motion unless you relate all that you learn, from people and from books, to your life in some way that makes sense to you. Ask questions about yourself: What am I really like? What do I want to be like? What really matters to me in my relationships with my family and my friends, in my studies and my work? What are my ultimate concerns? What difference will it make, in the kind of person I become, whether I learn to answer these questions or whether, sometime, I just stop asking them?

There are many teenagers like Dick. They worry about whether they have friends, whether they truly "belong" in the crowd, whether the crowd really wants them "in." They are anxious about whether they will make good grades and complete high school and college, whether they will have a happy marriage and a home of their own, and whether they will compete creditably in the adult world.

It is not surprising that teenagers tend to be preoccupied with their perplexities. From the early teens into the twenties, bodies are growing rapidly; teenagers feel emotions and impulses new to them. They are discovering that they no longer want to live as children. They want, fiercely, to be less dependent on others—but they are so sensitive to the opinions of others, so concerned about being accepted! What do people *really* expect of them? Earlier patterns of getting along with people no longer work. How do they learn new patterns?

As these worries multiply, teenagers handle them differently. When one teenager does not know what to do or say—or how to make himself behave as he feels he should, his worry becomes disguised. He forgets what specifically worried him; he knows only that he is worried. He becomes generally restless, confused, cynical—what's the use of required courses; what's the use of going to school at all? He's tired of learning. He grows indifferent—rebellious; he refuses to make plans for his future.

This teenager is attempting to handle his doubts and fears by despairing of himself—"I'm hopeless—what's the use?" He may "explain" this behavior by saying that "you have to give up several years of life to the government before you can think of your own future." Actually, he is afraid to face *any* future lest he prove inadequate to its demands.

A teen-age girl may try to resolve her fears about herself by redoubling her efforts to do "what is expected" of her at home and at school. However, redoubled effort may intensify inadequacy. Suppose that a girl actually does not possess as much academic ability as others in her class. In the competition for grades in school, her repeatedly low grades persistently remind her of her inferiority. This experience may destroy her ambition; or she may refuse to face her limitations and drive toward impossible goals.

Tackle the Job!

Worry about the kind of person he or she is or can be is so widespread among teenagers that it can be called normal. Despairing or disguising one's doubts and fears, however, is unprofitable. Everyone *can* do more than worry! Recognize your fears for what they are—fear of life, fear of growing up.

Such fear is difficult to express. You find it hard to talk about; you are not certain whether your friends feel as you do, so you are hesitant about betraying yourself. Don't be afraid. All teenagers will understand you. In fact, every intelligent adult all his life has a healthy respect for the power of this fear.

What is this fear of life? Technically, it should be called anxiety: for fear stems from a definite source which can be confronted and overcome. The anxiety teenagers feel is all-pervading. It has many origins. Some of it comes from a personal sense of not being able to meet the future. Your picture of yourself—your self-confidence—is threatened. You feel that you should be going in a hundred directions; instead, you cannot move at all. That's just the way Dick felt as he kept wondering, "What's wrong with me?"

If, like Dick, you recognize your fears as anxiety about life, you too will seek Dick's solution—to face today's prob-

16

lems today. The soundest preparation for that tomorrow —when you will be an adult—is to live adequately today. Do you feel doubtful and uncertain about what you do today? You can never know *the* future; but certain it is that you can gain confidence in *your* future only by gaining confidence in your "self." Are you unhappy about today's "self"? Make yourself into someone you like! Only genuine achievements can develop lasting self-respect!

What Is a Teenager?

SHARON was telling Ellen about taking care of her three-year-old cousin for several months in summer while his mother was in the hospital.

"You know, at first I felt sorry for myself—stuck with Martin. But you learn so much watching kids—things that help you understand people—and yourself! I used to wonder why some people our age were more friendly and interesting than others. Well, now I think all kids have curiosity—they could *all* grow up to be interesting—if they were encouraged!

"Take the way kids have to touch everything or put it in their mouths. That's the way they find out about things and about themselves too—that their thumb belongs to them; it hurts when they hit it—but it doesn't hurt them when they hit their stuffed rabbit. Kids are interested in exploring everything and in talking to everybody—when they're allowed to. Only some of them aren't allowed to— so they lose their curiosity and interest—and then they get to be pretty dull kids. Like Terry next door: our neighbor used to tie this four-year-old outside on a long rope around the tree most of the day—to keep him out of her way while she did housework—and to keep the house clean, she said. Usually he'd have only one or two playthings. He'd soon get bored. Then he'd cry awhile; then he'd go to sleep.

"Terry was a nice-looking little kid—or he would have been if it hadn't been for his eyes—he never looked anybody straight in the eyes. I used to think he was just sulky— then, when I knew him better, I decided he was scared of people. We'd go over and play with him sometimes and, really, when you got Martin and him together, Martin talked more, could do more things, and was lots more interesting at three than Terry at four. Yet, I'm sure that actually Martin wasn't any smarter. . . ."

"How could a kid of three be interesting?" Ellen asked.

"He always wanted to know about things—how they worked—would you help him 'try how'—he watched everything I did so intently; you know, it was flattering—and he loved people. He made friends with everybody. He was so different from Terry. That kid was afraid to try anything and always getting hurt when he did try. It was hard to make friends with him too. He would sit and hang his head, or, if his mother was around, would get in back of her whenever anyone new came along. It made his mother furious. She'd pull him out and try to make him 'talk like Martin.' "

"That's silly," Ellen said. "No two kids are alike."

"No, they couldn't be—not when they'd had different experiences, like these two. Martin couldn't help knowing that his parents loved him and thought he was a darling. They talked to him and were interested in what he wanted to do and to try. Martin was important in his family. Sometimes the little brat thought he was too important!

"Look at poor Terry! I don't mean that his parents were really bad parents. They fed him and clothed him nicely. But they seemed indifferent and unconcerned about him. They didn't spend much time with him—they shoved him off by himself. Then when he was afraid to try something Martin was doing, they'd make fun of him. What used to make me maddest was the way his mother would say, 'Speak up like Martin. Don't be such a dope.' "

Ellen interrupted, "Gosh, don't you feel sorry for a kid like that!"

"Yes," Sharon answered, "but look at the kids we know who are like that! It makes me realize what a teenager is— just Martin or Terry with a few years added and lots of the same old troubles!"

Your Self Is Always with You

How right you are, Sharon! No one's self is ready-made. Each of you acquires it gradually. It begins developing in infancy. As you noticed with Martin, long before a baby knows words, he learns the meaning of affection—or indifference, just by the way his parents or his brothers and sisters handle him. If they generally respond to his cries, gratify without too much delay his needs for food, comfort, and love, a baby usually feels comfortable and happy—until he learns to walk and tries to talk! Then he finds that he cannot reach things he wants, cannot do what he wants, often cannot make people understand what he wants. Demands are made on him; he is expected to respond to directions, to learn certain habits, to conform to his parents' and other people's wishes. His self begins to feel small, helpless, at the mercy of people bigger than he whom he must please if he wishes to be loved, approved of—sometimes, even fed. So he appraises himself as his parents appraise him; he *must* identify with them in order to feel that he is strong—like them. He considers himself a desirable, likable, and adequate person if they so consider him.

Fortunate is the small child who feels accepted and welcomed at home, who is given freedom, responsibilities, and opportunities—at his maturity level—to explore his environment, try out his abilities, learn about people and the world around him. This child develops a picture of himself as generally worthwhile, effective, and likable. His picture is substantially accurate because it is based on *actual* life experience.

How does someone develop a picture of himself as ineffective and unimportant? Unfortunately, if parents do not value a child, he can learn only to depreciate himself as they do; he considers himself a failure. When a child is unloved, what incentive is there to grow? Such a person cares little about controlling himself or responding to others. Even when he is mature physically, he remains an infant emotionally.

The infantile teenager is not necessarily a person neglected by his family. He may, in fact, have been overvalued or overindulged. The overvalued child cannot learn from his parents to value his "self," for they do not value it. To them, he may be a symbol, a promise of the fulfillment of cherished ideas of their own. They advertise this brilliant, beautiful, or gifted child. They may push him too early into competition with others; they may urge him at the cost of physical or nervous exhaustion to excel scholastically or in some specialized area like athletics, science, music, or dancing.

Such parents have grandiose ideas about a child, but little concern about *him* as an individual. When the child senses the fact that he has never been accepted and loved for what *he* is, he may become quarrelsome or stubborn in an attempt to *demand* from his parents the acceptance which most parents freely *give* to children. The parents, on the other hand, may discover that the child cannot fulfill their unrealistic ambitions, and may impatiently reject him, especially if a younger child with more promise comes along.

An overindulged child is at odds with himself. As he grows up, he becomes increasingly unhappy because he discovers that he is ineffective in facing his problems; he is often considered by people outside his family as a fairly unimportant, possibly not even likable, person. His parents had treated him as though he were all-important. Perhaps they wanted to "give him the best of everything." They made life easy. They covered up his mistakes; they excused him from responsibilities; they protected him from consequences of his wrong choices and decisions. What is more natural than that such a person expects the world to fall in his lap without effort on his part?

When he finds that it does not do so, he is filled with hostility toward his parents and with fear of others and the world. He is incapable of using his capacities because he was robbed of opportunity to develop them. In fact, he does not know what abilities he possesses because he never attempted anything on his own; he did only what his parents told him to do. He has had no practice in solving his problems or in developing and respecting his unique "self."

Teenagers know no other way of responding to people save the way they have experienced; you can't know what friendliness is, for example, unless sometime someone has been friendly with you. Accordingly, some teenagers have learned positive, others have learned basically negative attitudes toward people. Is it surprising that teenagers who have learned only negative attitudes attempt to satisfy their need for acceptance by bullying, by disparaging others, or by demanding always to be first or best?

The need to strike out at someone may persist in a person even when he is with people who would gladly accept him. Defensiveness may become *chronic* suspicion of other people's motives—you know teenagers who are always afraid someone is talking about them or criticizing them? Or it may become vindictiveness—trying to get other people into trouble, then leaving them "holding the bag." Again, it may develop into a habit of blaming others when things go wrong without considering one's own responsibility in the matter. Or it may go to other extremes: a teenager may try to buy friends and social acceptance with money or other bribes—or by being too, too good!

"Yes, I know people like that," Ellen says. "They're impossible. People who behave that way have no right to expect a decent person to try to be friendly, much less to like them. I just disregard them—try to pretend they're not even there. They're bad actors!"

"That's what I'd have said last year," Sharon interrupts Ellen thoughtfully. "Now I'm going to look at someone who acts like that and say 'the poor little kid next door grown up!' "

"What do you mean?" Ellen demands.

Sharon is talking in a faraway tone: "I can just see him. I'll bet, already, he feels that the world has let him down, that he's 'no good' and, it follows then, that other people are 'no good.' He can't put the feeling into words now—but when he's a teenager, he will. He'll probably talk about what a dope he is, how he's clumsy and sloppy and not handsome like other guys. He'll say all this, hoping he can inveigle someone into building him up. But no one will! Other teenagers will just be bored. So, when someone he'd hoped to cultivate dismisses him as the dope he said he was, a person like this just gets more unhappy—surer than ever that no one is any good and the world is unfriendly. He may decide that he'll either have to fight it or go it alone. I wonder if he'll ever realize that, as long as he can't believe in himself, he can't believe in anybody else. . . ."

What Are You Making of Your Self?

Suppose upon reading the last few pages you said to yourself smugly, "Yes, we seniors are having a course in psy-

chology. That's what I learned there, too. It's your parents'
fault if you're a mess."

Stop right there! Perhaps you do feel, not exactly rejected by your parents—but you're not as bright, as handsome, as good, or as popular as you wish—and maybe they
wish—you were. Or suppose you have awful parents—
your father drinks and there's always fighting. Or suppose
no one seems to care. Your "self" is made up of what your
parents and other people think about you and, if that isn't
so good, it's tough for you. But also *you* make yourself
what you are!

True, as a preschool child, you were with your parents
more than with anyone else. What they said to you and believed about you was almost all you knew. That's why early
feelings go deep; few other estimates are available. You
are too little and helpless to escape your home, so you absorb everything—parents' joys, sorrows, successes, failures,
humiliations and prejudices as these are expressed in their
attitudes toward you. Teenagers, however, are years removed from the preschool child.

Of course, your parents have deeply affected your "self."
For better or for worse? That's up to you! You are now old
enough to decide: what are you going to make of what happened to you early in life—of what is happening to you
daily during the hours you spend at home? Your feelings
about your home may be a combination of "I'm happy. I'm
relaxed. I can break down and tell my troubles and be
myself" or "Sometimes, I just can't seem to please them;
they think I'm not as good as my sister; I'm afraid to talk
things over with them. They try to understand—but then
they keep harping and nagging" or, rarely, "I just want to

get away. I don't want to be like them. I can't stand them and they can't stand me."

If your home has created and continues to create negative attitudes in you, what might you do? You might agree when, for example, your father vows that the world is out to "get you" and you have to fight people to avoid their giving you "a raw deal." You might sulk that everyone is against you and your family and out for himself; no one gives you a fair chance.

On the other hand, you might learn to understand how every adult, like every teenager, is molded by his experience. Some parents have had grim experiences—and no help in handling them. When today's adults, including your parents, were growing up, most of them did not know enough about how people get to be the way they are to recognize the places in their own lives where they might have made "a wrong turn." You, however, do know that even serious difficulties can be overcome. Regardless of how disastrous your past has been, it is possible, with professional help, to triumph over it. You can become so interested in learning what you must know in order to have your life turn out differently from your parents' that you waste no energy crying about what they did not do for you.

What you are now is dependent on *all* that has gone before in your life. Although your parents may still be the *dominant* influence in your life, how many hours do you spend away from home daily? Have you utilized this time for growth toward the "self" you are today? Many people, many situations, and many opportunities have come your way. Have you taken advantage of these resources to

26

further your development? What have you learned from your experiences?

How do *you* feel about the kind of person you are now: are you attractive, likable, a smart kid? Can you turn a hand at anything or are you someone with no looks or no personality whom people just "put up with"? Probably your estimate will be somewhere in between. To know *why* you feel a certain way, it is useful to understand that your estimate is the sum total of your past experiences and relationships with people. You learned that you were a certain kind of person partly *because people told you so.* Then, as a result of the way you reacted to people and to your experiences, you so judged yourself.

As you begin to understand how your present "self" came from your past, you can gauge how a future "self" will come from your present. This process may "get you in deep" sometimes in terms of early identifications and of all that happens inside you—beyond your conscious control and understanding. Certainly it is desirable to know when one is having deep-seated problems and to cooperate with the professional person from whom one seeks help. Fortunately, a comparatively small number of teenagers have *serious* difficulties, and this book makes no pretense of dealing with deep and complicated mechanisms which involve "the unconscious." Nor is it the purpose of this book to encourage you to look inside yourself for "problems." Introspection for its own sake is not rewarding! If things are going well with you, relax—enjoy being yourself!

On the other hand, even though you are not the victim of deep trouble, you may not be happy about yourself. Achieving one's best "self" is a long and arduous process; mistakes and fumbling are inevitable. Many teenagers have difficulties caused by undesirable types of behavior. Perhaps this book will convince you that you can learn to understand the origins of some behavior, that you can become capable of dealing with some of your conflicts and of so modifying and changing your behavior that you grow in self-understanding and in ability to handle life situations effectively. Thus you will "find" your most acceptable "self."

Obviously, if you want to know where you are going, you must know where you are—and what you are—because you as an adult will not be a new person, independent of your past. What you can expect of a future "self" depends largely on the kind of "self" you are now. Does this discourage you? Suppose you consider yourself "a mess" to date. Take heart! You will not remain today's "self."

Growth is inevitable. Should growth cease, life would cease. Think of physical growth as an example: pleasant as it may seem to remain a baby, no one remains one—physically, at least. You cannot delay the physiological and glandular changes which move you toward adulthood. The mere fact that you are living means that no part of you is ever static.

Growth of a "self" is inevitable too—but not automatic. Just as every cell in your body is changing constantly, so *you* are changing emotionally, mentally, and socially. Yet change does not necessarily mean growth. You must make it so. You must understand *how* you grow as a "self."

The very process of living forces you to confront certain important tasks at each level of your development. As you learn to solve each daily problem more effectively, you

28

gradually grow in understanding of all problems. Whenever you think a clearer thought, or face a difficult fact, or feel a deeper understanding, you have gained something, forever.

Still, your effectiveness will vary from time to time with different circumstances. Growth of a "self" proceeds by fits and starts. People cannot always be at their best; therefore, uninterrupted growth cannot be expected. Thus *each* person determines the rate and direction of *his own* growth. Each moves "on his own steam."

But move you will! So do not expect too much of yourself—or too little, but set yourself a goal: the creation of a self you'll like better than the one you're living with now. Then—get on with the work of creation! Wet paint signs cannot remain up indefinitely: difficulties should not block you too long; tasks cannot be permanently evaded by dreaming about how much happier you'd be or how much more chance you'd have in another family, classroom, school, or neighborhood—with more money, more clothes, more brains, or a car!

What if you haven't a clear goal—you just feel, somehow, dissatisfied with yourself? That's very hopeful. Discontent need not be unhappiness, frustration, misery; it can be "divine unwillingness" to be less than it is possible for you to be. Today's problems are not a sign of past ineffectiveness or weakness; they are a springboard to future challenges. Some people grow with these challenges; others only swell— in anger or frustration!

That's How You "Got That Way"

LEARNING to understand yourself is not a matter of chronological age. Let's look at Mike. At sixteen, Mike is not adult. Yet, if maturity is the growing ability to be honest about oneself and one's feelings, to face one's problems, to make choices and abide by their consequences, Mike is far more mature than many adults.

Mike's parents fight a great deal. His father often starts it. But then, his mother does "egg him on"—she seems to have a gift for throwing up to him that he can't keep a job more than a few months, that he drinks too much, and that he's "always brawling" with someone. Mike wonders, as he listens, what his mother gains by her methods. Mike feels sorry for both of them. He knows that each one is unhappy. He tries to be as pleasant as possible; they both care about him—in their way. They've tried often to be kind to him.

However, Mike "gets too low" staying around home, so he's found himself a job in a gas station. When he was younger, a teacher who was a scout leader got him into the Boy Scouts. He says the three summers he spent at a scout camp and the meetings they had in the teacher's home helped him to see that not all people acted toward one another as they did in his family; home life *could* be different. Mike has stuck with the scouts; he has worked with the teacher as assistant scoutmaster ever since he was fourteen when the teacher "graduated" Mike's troop and started over again with a bunch of seven-year-old boys.

Mike demonstrates what is meant by making the most of what you have. Moreover, Mike knows that, as he takes on the form of an adult physically, society will judge him by what he is—a person more or less competent to meet life. Society's appraisal will not take into consideration the adequacy or inadequacy of what his parents did for him.

Mike has learned that understanding yourself is not resignation or quiet submission to fate. Mike could have tried to shunt off responsibility for what he became by saying that his parents had given him no example and no home. He saw his mother excusing herself for what she was by blaming his father for what he had done to her. In turn, his father blamed his mother for "a disposition that drives a man to drink."

Mike, however, decided that *he* had some responsibility for his own life. Instead of moaning that others were guilty for what they had done to him, Mike reasoned that he himself would be guilty if he used the character and actions of others to excuse his own failures. He is willing to face his inner limitations and outer restrictions so that, knowing his limits, he does not feel bound by them. On the contrary, knowing what he cannot do leaves him free to develop his possibilities in areas where he can succeed.

Mike respects himself *as he is;* this step is basic in helping others to feel friendly and comfortable with him. Mike understands that he himself has limitations and problems, but, in spite of these, he knows himself to be a worthwhile kind of guy—one on whom he, and others, can depend. Consequently, Mike will accept other people's limitations, yet see them as "good guys"; he will respect their achievements and believe in their sincerity. People will respond with their best to Mike because he expects the best of them.

Mike understands the essential quality in living—that today's attitudes, choices, and actions actually determine the direction of his life. Mike, therefore, is developing what all teenagers want—faith in themselves, confidence in others, and ability genuinely to relate to and communicate with others. Thus, day by day, Mike is building his future. If you *set your own house in order*, you can trust the future because you are able to take whatever time and circumstances may bring!

Your Inheritance

Everyone begins life with some basic equipment, although the repertoire of inborn tendencies, abilities, and all that is inherent in one's make-up differs from person to person. In other words, you are partly the product and result of your inheritance, your habits, and your attitudes. Your "self" is regulated by these factors just as surely as by the already-discussed experiences of your environment.

We are what we are partly because of our biological inheritance: tall parents tend to have tall children; blond, blue-eyed parents to have blond, blue-eyed children like themselves. Some people inherit tendencies to certain diseases. We inherit certain types of temperaments: passive or eager, quick or slow, fretful or placid. Some people inherit greater *capacity* than others to think and act intelligently.

We become what we are partly because of the situation into which we are born: the habits and standards of our families, the social customs of our friends and neighbors, the outside forces affecting our families and our communities. These are our inheritance just as are our physical characteristics. Many teenagers do not know how to employ this broad definition of inheritance in understanding themselves. They are too close to themselves to see themselves.

They may be able to look at others: Susan Smith—sure, I can see how she got that way. No wonder she whines and has temper tantrums when she doesn't get her way. She's so spoiled—the only girl in that family of boys, the baby sister—they wait on her hand and foot, give her what she wants before she's finished asking for it. Bill Brown— yes, it's easy to understand why he always fights to be "on top." His father drinks too much and gets in trouble. Bill and his mother are determined to prove to the world that

Bill is not like that; in fact, that he is better than most people. But me, I don't behave like that!

Your Attitudes

The way any teenager thinks and acts is basically influenced by his parents, his family, his "gang," friends, neighbors, and public opinion in general. The teenager knows that certain people expect certain forms of behavior from him. If he wants them to like him, his behavior reflects their expectations. Sometimes the teenager *wants* to copy these people; sometimes he consciously determines not to be like them. In either case, what they are and what they believe play an important part in determining the kind of person he is.

A teenager gains confidence in his "self" as people important to him judge him as a worthwhile person. Therefore, he makes an effort to develop the kind of "self" people seem to expect him to be. In other words, he acts out *the role* assigned him. He aims to please. Cast in a role, the teenager plays it, whether or not he is aware of what he is doing! It is not so much the example of others which he imitates as the reflection of himself in their eyes and the echo of himself in their words!

Suppose the teenager lives in a community where adults— and his "gang"—look upon teenagers as crazy, mixed-up kids, unpredictable nitwits, or vandals: these attitudes toward him may reinforce such characteristics in him if he tends toward this behavior. The clothes this teenager may then choose to wear, the language he may use, the movies he may see, the books and magazines he may read—all may foster this conception of himself. He may even get into trouble with the police. He may not like himself in this role. But it is difficult to overcome the tendency to shape ourselves in the image other people have of us.

For example, in a family, three people whom we shall call Helen, Jim, and Sally are, unconsciously, assigned different roles. Jim is visualized by the family as a scatterbrain, a humorist, the life of the party; Sally is considered the thinker—a dependable individual who never forgets anything, always does what is expected of her, is always kind and courteous, always thinks before she speaks; Helen is the baby who needs to be waited on and protected. What can they do? They may resent and fight the role in which they are cast, or fall into the role and act as expected, or figure out how to assert their real selves.

On campus or in school, one individual may be visualized by a teacher as "a discipline problem," another as "a good kid," another as "a brain," another as "a cocky guy." Sometimes parents confirm a teenager in a certain role because they want a baby; they cannot allow a child to grow up. Parents and teachers may need to bolster their own egos by having a popular son, a "good" daughter, a brilliant student.

A teenager's behavior is especially influenced by other teenagers. Social pressures—the way he and his friends see themselves—explain many a teenager's habits, attitudes, and actions. Suppose that a teenager, in the course of a day, becomes a part of several groups, groups so diverse as to expect from him different types of behavior; for example, his family, his employer, and his gang. What will the teenager do? He will respond to the standards of the group with which he most closely identifies himself; he will assume the role they assign him. Many teenagers tend to develop the kind of "self" that *their friends seem to expect of them.* Parents, schools, and employers do not always understand this. A teenager himself may not realize that his friends' expectations explain his "Everybody's doing it" or "You don't understand." These pressures operate beyond the limits of his awareness. He "just does"—or does not do— certain things! He takes these expectations for granted.

Moreover, the way teenagers see their behavior in the gang is sometimes different from the way parents or teachers see it. If teachers and parents misunderstand what teenagers are up against as they behave as they feel they must in order to remain "in" with the gang, teenagers accuse adults of letting them down, of being unfair and unjust, of judging the inconspicuous many by the conspicuous few "because you simply don't trust us." That parents and teachers cannot always understand does not mean that they do not *try* to understand.

On the other hand, the gang may not understand one another. They may be amazed at a quiet boy's clowning and silliness because he is "so good" at home and at school. The gang needs to learn that this boy behaves as "expected" at home or at school; he must be "like that" in order to survive. He is "so good," not because he wants to be all the time, but because he feels he must assume the role assigned him by parents and teachers. With the gang, he "breaks out" in completely opposite behavior because he feels free to experiment with them. Such a boy is trying to find out what he is really like.

People may continue all their lives to do what is expected

of them. Some merely repeat a role they learned to play early in life because it got them what they wanted, or at least, avoided what they did not want.

Generally, such a person does not understand why he behaves as he does. Consciously, he knows only that he reacts to people according to the way he *feels* about them. He feels annoyed with some; others make him belligerent, sulky, or stubborn. Of some people he is tolerant; with others, he is cooperative or enthusiastic. Pressed for reasons why he behaves in these different ways, he probably will give *logical* explanations for his actions. But these may not be the *real* reasons.

Suppose such a person is introduced to someone. Something about the new acquaintance vaguely brings back an early experience. Perhaps he is reminded of an uncle who, sometime in his childhood, punished him harshly. From this half-forgotten memory, fear, hurt pride, and humiliation are reawakened. The new acquaintance is not responsible for these feelings; yet he is snubbed or coldly treated—as though he personally caused these feelings. The same dislike, originally and logically felt for the uncle, is felt for this new person.

An adult may act toward friends, toward employers, and toward persons in authority as he originally acted toward his parents. If he was afraid of his parents, if he copied them, if he rebelled against them, if they were "pals" or people he respected and liked to talk to, he may so treat friends, employers, and people in authority.

Another adult may treat friends or fellow-workers as he treated his brothers and sisters. If in his family he learned friendliness, cooperation, the sharing of privileges and responsibilities, he will approach other people with these attitudes. On the other hand, if, as the oldest child, he exercised authority and was looked up to, he may try to dominate friends and colleagues or want them to respect his dignity. If he tried to outdo brothers and sisters, he may consider himself in competition with friends and colleagues. If he developed jealousy because parents distributed their love unequally, he may become jealous of friends and co-workers.

A person's behavior toward the opposite sex also is influenced by what he learned at home. If either sex was especially waited upon, he may expect a similar attitude in the world outside. In fact, in some marriages, the wife is more a mother than a bride, the husband more a father than a spouse. If a teenager is learning now that a member of his or her sex must protect his own rights, then, as an adult, he may continue to fight for what he wants; he may tend to quarrel over trifles. On the other hand, if he learns that men and women talk over all problems or share what they have with one another, he will have difficulty with the person who is accustomed to seeing one sex take orders from the other, do all the housework, or have no control of family finances. Is this sufficient evidence to show why teenagers need to understand how attitudes affect behavior?

Your Habit Pattern

Your inheritance and your attitudes go a long way in explaining how you "got that way." Habits are important too. Everyone was taught to respond in certain ways to certain situations. We cling to childhood habits because we feel comfortable with them. Most of us prefer to move in the old familiar ways of doing things. Familiar habits may not always be efficient; but they give a sense of security—we "know how" to do what is expected. Everyone needs reassurance in a world changing as rapidly as ours. Moreover, everyone is a little afraid of the new and unknown!

Therefore, when a person is forced to change a cherished habit too quickly, he argues and grows hostile. No one can *force* change in another. If there is to be genuine change, a person must want to change because *he himself* doesn't like what he is doing now. The first step in changing a habit is examining it critically: what exactly did I do? How did I learn to behave this way? Why did I think I needed to do this?

Sometimes a teenager's conviction of his own "righteousness" prevents this honest evaluation. For example, if someone is angry about a criticism of himself, he may become so occupied with the "wrong" done him that he does not see what *he* did which annoyed his critic. He feels only an impulse to "get back at" the person who criticized him. This person needs to look *inside himself*.

Since growth proceeds by fits and starts, everyone makes some mistakes and wrong moves. The teenager who hopes to eliminate his negative attitudes and bad habits will learn to examine his behavior to find out *why* he resorted to second-rate behavior. Then he will plan new ways of behaving which will be more satisfying to him and more acceptable to other people. For example, a teenager who wants to like people whom he now dislikes may discover that old hurts and insecurities—sometimes social expectations or fears of "what people will say"—explain his prejudiced behavior. He determines to modify his behavior. As he faces new experiences without fear, he begins to resolve his fears. At the same time, he finds that his new acquaintances are interesting—and lots of fun.

What Do You Really Want?

Every "self" is unique. No one can tell you what *you* really want. Everyone must understand his basic human needs. Everyone must learn to face his limitations without fear so that he can be comfortable with himself. Finally everyone must find something he can believe in, so that his life seems to him to have some purpose and direction.

By basic human needs, psychologists mean that everyone needs food, rest, air, and activity. In addition, all human beings want love and affection, security and a feeling of worth, success and the joy of achievement, new experiences and relief from monotony.

Sometimes these needs are difficult to reconcile one with another. Teenagers frequently want, simultaneously, to feel loved by and close to some people—like their family and friends; yet they want to feel independent of them, able to stand "on their own." Teenagers want to feel that they are unique, with a unique contribution to make to the world—yet they want to be accepted by people who are important to them. It takes confidence in oneself, the development of all one's possibilities, and genuine courage to learn to meet these conflicting needs.

To develop self-confidence. Ellen is talking about Sharon: "She is so spontaneous and sincere. She can always think of something to say to make people comfortable. I wish I had her confidence. I get embarrassed. I guess I'm too

40

self-conscious." Ellen is observant. She realizes that sincerity and spontaneity in expressing one's feelings are evidence that one can count on one's self. The person who responds in each situation with actions appropriate to that situation shows that he knows what he wants to do, what he can do, and what he is able to expect of himself. Some psychologists say that such a person has developed "self"-consciousness or self-awareness.

To most teenagers, unfortunately, self-consciousness means shyness and embarrassment. "Shouldn't I forget myself?" Ellen asks nervously. Actually, "self"-consciousness is the opposite of morbid "looking-in-at-yourself"; it is the capacity to see yourself as others see you—to look *out* at yourself as though you were another person seeing you for the first time. If Ellen is embarrassed, she stands outside herself, yes—but only to measure herself, to try to get other people to reassure her about herself. A shy, embarrassed person is a stranger to herself; she is afraid to claim herself. No one can be spontaneous and wholehearted if she cannot believe in or depend on herself!

If Ellen is to develop confidence in herself, she must see herself accurately—all of herself—her limitations as well as her possibilities. If she is to know what to expect of herself, she must be able to assume responsibility for all she sees. It is difficult to do this, partly because much that explains behavior goes on beyond one's awareness. Many of us can *see* other people—we know that Bill is a fighter and Susan a whiner—but we cannot *see* ourselves. Unconsciously, we have hidden parts of ourselves. Then, because we do not see the way we behave, we do not hold ourselves responsible for our behavior. The more parts of ourselves we keep hidden away, the more we are frightened by what is hidden.

Ellen can be helped to get out of hiding her imperfections, mistakes, and failures—the parts of herself she "can't bear to think about." The more of herself she can look at without fear, the more surely can she begin to rely on herself; as she recognizes that she is a many-sided person, feelings of inadequacy in some areas will inevitably be balanced by feelings of self-worth.

Suppose, however, that a teenager feels that he is entirely inadequate. This may not be true; but he *sees* himself like this because this is what people important to him in his early life saw. A boy expressed such a feeling when he said his "self-confidence was shot." Like most teenagers, he needs assurance from people whom he values. When he is deeply discouraged, he needs to talk over his feelings with friends in a "bull session," with a parent, teacher, or other older person, or with a professional counselor.

In any one of these experiences, a teenager learns to see himself more accurately. He receives help in locating the problems which explain his unhappiness; he gains sufficient understanding to accept what he cannot change in himself and courage to change what is necessary to ensure his self-acceptance. Then he needs experiences—many, many opportunities to prove to himself that these people are right—that he *is* a worthwhile and adequate person. Thus, gradually, he changes his poor estimate of himself to one more worthy of his abilities. He begins to accept himself and to build confidence in himself because he *sees himself* differently.

Self-acceptance is different from self-centeredness or self-pride, which may indicate that you are thinking too constantly, too highly, or at least *unrealistically* about yourself. Egotism does not originate in greater consciousness of "self" or in feelings of self-confidence. On the contrary, it commonly covers feelings of inadequacy.

Self-acceptance or self-love is necessary and good. It is the opposite of selfishness. In fact, self-love is a prerequisite for loving others. Only the teenager who has had sound experience of his own worth has a basis for acting generously toward his neighbor.

Self-knowledge also casts out fear. Knowing what you are and what you can expect of yourself widens your control of your "self." With expanded power comes capacity to be spontaneous—to "let yourself go"—a phrase used often without realization of what it implies! Actually, you allow yourself to be natural only when you trust yourself. For example, in carrying on a conversation, playing a game of tennis, or driving a car, the less confident you are, the more tense you are; the tighter you keep your grip on the wheel, the racket, or the conversation. With confidence, you relax; you are conscious that "you" are in control.

To use your possibilities. Conscious that "you" are the directing agent in all you do, examine, each day, what you have made of yourself. Do you "produce" what is expected at home, at school, with friends, or on the job? Toward what kind of "self" are *today's* experiences moving you?

Scorn no possibility. Whether you learned today to make yourself more attractive, to throw a pass in football, to gain a friend, to study more effectively, or to play a new piece on the piano—every honest and responsible expression of your powers will increase your sense of achievement, will bring deep satisfaction, and will develop faith in yourself as a fairly successful manager of your own affairs.

Can you "pull your weight" in a group yet not be dependent on their opinion? When you differ from them, can you calmly and rationally explain your position? Do you make some decisions in terms of your own convictions and interests? Can you disagree with people without being disagreeable?

Are you learning to get along with people whether you like them or not? Are you judging people on their own merits rather than according to your prejudices? Do you help people if you can? Do you appreciate their interest in you—even when it takes the form of constructive criticism?

Do you generally face your perplexities instead of fearing, fighting, or avoiding them? Can you discriminate between possible choices and actions? What responsibilities have you assumed—or escaped—today? Are you learning what you can expect of yourself, then setting goals in accordance with your ability? Are you growing less fearful of using your intellectual powers lest you be teased as a "brain"? Do you plan your future in terms of lessons learned from past mistakes? Or do you fear both the past and the "terrible things" that may happen in some vague future?

A teenager who does not use his possibilities will gradually lose his sense of being a person—just as, if he never used his arms and legs, he would lose sensation in them; they would wither. Unused potentialities turn inward and cause a *person* to wither and despair. Anyone who has been unable to be or do what he dreamed of being or doing is deeply disappointed in himself no matter with what "good reasons" or excuses he explains that "I'd be different if only...."

Developing your possibilities, obviously, implies self-discipline, willingness to face facts, ability to relate to other human beings, and discrimination between various sets of values. The latter sometimes implies destruction. Suppose a teenager finds that he can no longer believe something he formerly accepted. He feels guilty. It is like abandoning part of himself. Possibly he must also hurt someone in the process of moving to new ways of thinking, acting, or relating to people. This is what happened to Wayne.

Wayne decided at summer camp that doctoring just wasn't for him—actually, he hadn't ever felt right about it. But his father was so wrapped up in *his* practice that Wayne had really believed that both of them would, one day, share that practice. Yet, all the time, he'd felt nauseated at thoughts of blood and sick people. In fact, he just didn't care too much about people, he admitted to himself in camp. He was happiest when he was tramping the woods, somewhat ahead of the rest, collecting leaf specimens, or staying awake nights "reading the sky" at outpost camp.

Wayne supposed he'd soon have to tell his family how he felt. He knew that his father would be disappointed. What he dreaded most, though, was that his father would say that Wayne was too young to know his own mind. He wondered if he *was* doing the right thing to abandon doctoring —and an assured practice—when, he admitted, he really had no clear alternative in mind. Yet Wayne felt deeply that changing his mind about doctoring was right. At the same time, he was afraid to change his mind. He felt almost

45

as though, if he changed too much, he might not be himself.

All teenagers have conflicting feelings when they find themselves thinking differently and wanting to act differently from their parents—whether the issue is their life-work or their beliefs about politics, religion, the inferiority of some race or nationality, or any issues about which their parents feel strongly. Any teenager confronted with the necessity for reversing the trend of his thoughts *is* frightened. Everyone fears leaving the old for the untried new.

Nevertheless, everyone must either go forward or sacrifice freedom to grow. Repeated refusals to change one's mind result in inability to face new facts or to initiate a new set of actions in keeping with new facts. Consider what would happen to a person who never changed his position physically; he would become rigid. If one never changes one's mind, it becomes rigid; one is "frozen in position."

The rigid person, be he eighteen or eighty, cannot bear change. He becomes anxious if things are not arranged in the order in which he learned them or if he does not know all the answers. So he shuts himself up with his answers and rituals—which are not to be questioned. He hopes, by changing nothing, to avoid life's uncertainties. He will not succeed. In fact, the blind conformist finally becomes unable to distinguish between what "he" is and what the world tells him he should be. A person's real "self" needs to be left reasonably free so that he may, increasingly, grow aware of his "self" as the person who makes his decisions and who acts.

As Wayne grows in ability to think and act for himself, he will replace old goals with new values. At first, he will be frightened at the prospect of standing alone for something he believes instead of doing what he is told. Some teenagers, in this stage of development, volubly defend their actions—trying to persuade their parents of their "right" to be themselves. All the time, many parents are rejoicing that a "self" is developing—although they may not always like all its manifestations!

Some teenagers never get beyond talking. Incidentally, by their argumentativeness, they admit that the authorities they address still seem all-powerful to them; they imply a feeling of guilt at daring to break away. Teenagers ranting loudest about wanting the outward trappings of freedom betray lack of inner freedom. They know that, as they deny others the right to make the laws of their lives, they must replace these laws by others equally firm which they have worked out for themselves. Yet they are afraid to accept responsibility for their own actions, thoughts, judgments, values, loves, and hates.

However, as teenagers become increasingly able to develop "on their own," they become—outwardly at least—more self-confident and poised. Naturally, everyone, all his life, has some inner doubts. But these do not make one obnoxiously aggressive or overbearing. A confident person does not need constantly to prove his worth, to excuse himself, or to shield himself from anxiety. He does not merely reflect people around him. He neither retreats into unproductive dreams nor resorts to activity for the sake of activity; he does not rely on "busyness" to make him feel alive and important. He is not "pushed around" by unconscious forces.

A self-confident person knows what he is doing! "You" face yourself as you really are; you look at what time has made of you to date and determine what time shall do in the future. You do not wait for something big and significant and "terrible" which you can battle. You try to move forward every day to a slightly better hold on the task of fulfilling your particular possibilities. In building a "self," what happens to you in life is not nearly as important as how you bear what happens and what you learn from it!

To face life with courage. Trying anything new always involves anxiety. Often you ask fearfully, "Can I succeed? What if I fail?" You want new friends, new experiences, new achievement. But the more you seek to realize your possibilities, the more capacity for overcoming fear you must develop. "Yes, I'd love to, I can, I'll try," says one part of you, while another part of you hesitates and asks fearfully, "Can you? Dare you try? Will you make a fool of yourself? What will 'they' say?" Your anxiety is, in part, desire for something you dread. Everyone wants to move ahead to realize his possibilities, yet everyone fears to do so. Therefore, everyone feels anxious sometimes.

No matter how old you become, trying something new will always involve anxiety. Someone may say "No" when you say "Yes"; someone may say "You may get hurt" when you say "Let me try." Choices are always accompanied by responsibility for the choices. You may have to clash with, even defy, important people in your life to win some opportunities to grow. You may have to withstand threats: "Choose to do that if you wish, but abide by the consequences."

The first-grader leaving home for school needs courage to let go the familiar. The child making his first friend outside the family must have courage to trust himself to an-

48

other. The teenager, a responsible person making a decision unpopular with his parents, needs courage consciously to stand alone, without the protection of his parents. Even a teenager whose parents say "Make up your own mind" feels alone. He is accustomed to the comfortable feeling of having his decisions made. At first he feels powerless in this new situation, while adults seem strong and sure of themselves. Normally, however, a teenager—in spite of his fears of growing up—is able to take every step from dependence on his parents to an independent "self" if he is aware of his parents' love—not coddling!—and sufficient healthy support so that he is not required to stand alone before he is prepared to do so. Such courage arises from a sense of dignity and self-esteem.

A teenager's courage is evidenced in willingness to move from parental dependence toward that genuine independence which he shows in growing capacity to take over direction of his own life. Immature teenagers think that merely *desiring* freedom, independence, and other adult prerogatives will transform them, spontaneously, into free, independent adults. Mature teenagers know that you *develop capacities* for freedom and independence only if, day by day, you dare to meet new situations constructively, if you continuously master new skills and build new resources inside yourself, if you bravely make decisions and abide by their consequences. Courage is necessary in every step of this process.

Courage is not rashness; rashness often covers anxiety. Courage is not a display of heroics. In fact, to assume a posture of open defiance, to fight or to risk physical pain often requires less courage than to make a decision which you think is right, but which will make enemies among your friends and associates or risk your parents' disapproval. Courage implies standing on your convictions, not defiantly or in retaliation for some imagined wrong, but simply because you want to believe in and stand for something. It is the opposite of automaton conformity.

Real courage is an inward quality; it is a way of relating yourself to your potentialities. It is willingness to overcome the anxiety inevitably aroused in you as you face "the alarming possibility of being able" to be or to do something. In other words, recognition of your possibilities is your recompense for confronting your fears. Courage is the price you pay to create a free, independent self.

It Takes a Heap of Living!

You are the product of many generations. You are the result of what your inheritance has made you, of what your parents and other people have made you, of what you have wanted for yourself and have made of yourself. You represent a heap of living!

Since your origins are so complex, it will also *take* a heap of living with your "self" before you will feel that you know your way around! It is not surprising that, sometimes, you are confused about yourself—or that parts of you sometimes dislike other parts. Behavior which you regret or of which you are ashamed—actions which you would rather not admit —"creep up on you." Because you don't understand why you behaved like this—you "didn't mean to"—you feel that you cannot depend on yourself.

In order that such experiences do not threaten your confidence in yourself, you need to know that all of us act "badly" sometimes. True, some people's behavior is self-defeating and blatantly destructive. These people are disturbed and need professional help. Most of us, however, can learn to understand why we act as we do and how we can change. Behavior is not something mysterious which happens to you in spite of yourself. Keep on trying to understand the "why"!

You Are Many People

You, like most teenagers, probably feel that it is difficult to understand yourself because you have so many selves. You are a different person in different places. You respond differently to different people. You have different attitudes toward yourself.

Sometimes what you think of yourself is more what you want to be than what you are. Possibly, you give plausible excuses for doing something you ought not to do. Therefore, in initial stages of trying to understand yourself, you are doubtlessly confused, even unhappy about yourself.

One bewildered teenager asks, "Why do I change so?" Life seems to be a shifting pattern of attitudes toward himself and toward others: for example, sometimes this teenager thinks adults idiotic and stupid. He has ventured to say that he does not feel the same as they about something and they have pushed him aside, told him that he is too young to be consulted. He knows that, though they tell him to keep his mouth shut, that does not stop him from having opinions. At such times, he feels strongly that adults don't understand him; they don't realize that he is much more sensitive and mature than they could ever dream. Consequently, he is furious with them.

A few moments later, he may be conscience-stricken *because* he is so full of rage at them. He needs their love and devotion. He yearns to have them understand him and he wants to understand them. If he is honest, even as he accuses them of not understanding him, he admits to himself that he does not understand them either.

Gradually, he becomes aware of the fact that their feelings about him are as complicated as his feelings; moreover, that often they are deeply worried about difficulties of their own. His rage turns to sympathy for them. It *is* understandable, then, that they have been irritable with him. Perhaps, he tells himself, he has taken their irritation too seriously; he has become offended too easily. Thus, he became more aggravating to them—which behavior, in turn, made both him and them more unhappy.

Every teenager has had this experience. Everyone can remember times when his feelings seemed to swing, almost unpredictably, from one extreme to another. You yourself may recall some occasion when you felt very warm and close to your parents because they had just helped you "out of a jam." A few hours later, you found yourself feeling ex-

tremely hostile—they "just don't trust me." Possibly you
wanted to do something which they would not allow—and
you did it anyway. You almost hated them—actually because you felt conscience-stricken about having gone counter
to their desires!

You also shift frequently in your attitudes toward the
gang. Sometimes you feel safe and happy because they
provide fun and friendship; then, if they get you into trouble
with other people important to you, you become fearful of
their influence over you, resentful of your dependence on
them, and angry with them because "they" made a fool of
you.

In most life situations, many attitudes are balanced. Occasionally, however, everyone becomes overbalanced in one
direction or another—often in one's attitudes toward relatively unimportant matters. For example, sometimes teenagers overstress the importance of certain behavior, such
as wearing skirts the right length, making the first team,
using the right fork, living on the right street. And they
think that people who do not vehemently agree with them
"just do not understand"!

Although everyone's behavior changes and shifts frequently, a certain personality pattern is characteristic of
each person. You can recognize, almost foretell, how a
given person will meet joy, sorrow, failure, success, compromise. One teenager may be accurately described as someone who is generally dependent, warm and affectionate, generally courageous, optimistic, and confident. Another teenager may be fearful and timid, somewhat anxious and afraid
to assert himself; another may be nagging and critical;
while still another is blatantly independent, self-centered,

54

and demanding. Under stress—when a teenager must face the consequences of some rash act, some illness or financial trouble or sorrow—his temperament may change temporarily. He may become more dependent, less affectionate toward outsiders, but more affectionate toward his family and intimate friends; or he may become more withdrawn— or openly hostile.

Your Behavior Is Caused

Everyone displays a variety of behavior, and everyone's behavior means something. You don't wake up some morning and begin behaving in a certain way without cause; there is always a "because." You do not suddenly become a hostile, cooperative, independent, loving, or hateful person; you act in these ways "because" of things that happened to you in the past or that motivate you in the present.

Most behavior is fairly adequate when it is interpreted correctly. Moreover, most behavior is normal. Normality covers a wide range. True, not all behavior you observe in others would be comfortable for *you;* and sometimes you tend to accept as normal only behavior which corresponds closely enough to your own standards to make *you* feel comfortable! Then you pass judgment! Anyone behaving differently is an odd ball!

Some behavior is learned behavior. A teenager may repeat certain ways of thinking, feeling, or acting from habit or because he once achieved his ends by behaving in this particular fashion. We observed in a previous chapter that a person may behave in certain ways because he feels that certain behavior is expected of him. Another person may not even *see* that he is behaving in a certain way—much less *un-*

derstand why he does so! He may be aware only that he *feels* this way.

Much behavior recurs because it fills a basic need. Everyone must have sufficient security, love, success, and new experience to make him feel that he is a worthwhile person. To a large degree, behavior is explained as some teenagers frankly admit: "I wanted to be liked"; "I wanted to be a success"; "I wanted to see what it felt like"; "I wanted the gang to consider me a good sport." Everyone must satisfy those needs; no one can say "Who, me?" and pretend to be unaffected by such desires.

To understand behavior, one must keep the goals in mind: each person wants to feel worthwhile, likable, successful, able courageously to face life, and to make the most of his possibilities. To reach these goals, everyone has *himself* to deal with; he must do the best he can with his *own* strengths and weaknesses, his *own* feelings of pride and shame, adequacy and inadequacy. Given time, patience, courage, and understanding support, most teenagers *can* learn gradually to penetrate beyond their alibis, face their real fears and doubts about themselves, finally *see* and *respect* their true selves.

The ways of behaving with which individuals experiment in their attempts to reach these goals are legion. Some ways are effective; others are second rate. It is more difficult for some people than for others to face their fear and doubt, shame, guilt, or inadequacy. Some people's behavior shows that they are fighting this admission in every way they can; others avoid or evade facing the whole truth about themselves. Some people resort to behavior which seems contrary to their own best interests. You know how you look ques-

56

tioningly at someone who has done something which, to you, appears shortsighted? Puzzled, you ask yourself, "Where is *that* getting him?"

Let us examine some less desirable behavior in order to try to understand why people behave like that. You have seen teenagers loudly rebelling, stridently "bossing" everyone around, being too, too good, whining, crying, or feigning illness, indulging in too obvious horseplay or temper tantrums, blaming the world for a raw deal, making other people the goat, being jealous or a know-it-all. You may even have seen some gambling, drinking, or taking drugs.

Some psychologists call these behavior patterns "defense mechanisms"; they say people are defending themselves against admitting inferiority or anxiety or discomfort. Certain of these defense mechanisms take the form of direct action—of attack on others. On the other hand, people also "defend" themselves by avoiding situations, people, or problems. No matter what the specific behavior—these are the scared people!

Some people fight their fears. Let us look first at the fighters—the attackers. Are they fearful—the bullies, the show-offs, the know-it-alls, the gossips, the ones who get what they want by temper tantrums, nasty cracks and sarcasm, defying authority, or even stealing? Such actions *do* betray fear.

If a person feels that he is not equal to a situation, he may threaten or otherwise attempt to terrify anyone who tries to make him face this situation. If he indulges in rages and other violent outbursts, he merely advertises the fact that he is "mad" because he's been given a job too big for him or because he thinks he is not being sufficiently appreciated.

Bullying is a cover for fear; the fact that the bully is a coward at heart is common knowledge. Equally true is the fact that the inferior person is a braggart. He who constantly demands the limelight in order to tell you how wonderful he is actually repeats himself in order to reassure himself. If he were certain that he was a worthwhile person, he would not have to tell you so often how wonderful he is! Even the show-off who resorts to horseplay, dirty stories, showing his muscles (the girl show-off shows her legs) is afraid that other people do not like him, so he'll at least force them to pay attention to him! However, he would much prefer to have you like him than look at him.

The know-it-all who is most dogmatic and intolerant in his opinions is least sure of himself. If he were sure, he would not have to impress you with his infallibility. He may merely repeat prejudices he has heard. Or he may be implying that any thing, any ideas, or anybody who is new or strange is open to suspicion, therefore to be fought or avoided. A know-it-all fears the unknown. He cannot seek or welcome new experiences, people, or ideas because he is afraid that he cannot cope with them successfully.

Such fear is often the real reason that gossip and rumor are spread about an individual new to a school or community —especially if one of the gossips feels that his or her status at school, in the gang, or on the team is threatened by the newcomer. On the other hand, fear is also an explanation of the reason some people cling to one or two friends and, too often, demand perfection of their hapless victims.

As some people hazard an opinion or suggest a course of action, they demand that their ideas be accepted at once. They have not learned to wait for what they want. They cannot control their desires; in fact, they grow hysterical if the achievement of their wishes is postponed. Anyone who always gets his way by loudly demanding what he wants when he wants it is frightened; he needs to have others pay attention to his wishes because he himself is not certain that his desires are important.

A fearful person may also embrace sudden change, yet resist any control. He may slavishly follow every fad and new idea. He does not know what he wants; therefore he cannot depend on himself. He avoids the *necessity* of depending on himself by depending, in continuous and rapid succession, on the *new* things his group thinks up.

A bossy person is sometimes one who is so busy telling other people what to do or talking about what others should be doing that he neatly avoids work himself. Thus, he never has to face the fact that actually he is afraid he "wouldn't do so well"—he might even be afraid that "he'd make a fool of himself."

Rebellion against other people may actually be the pent-up fear and rage of teenagers who, from childhood on, have had too much expected of them. They have been so frequently hurt or humiliated that they think they aren't worth much. They hit out at the world which has hurt them; they have "chips on the shoulder." Sometimes they become sarcastic and bitter; at other times, they boast that they don't care *what* people think of them. Yet they do care —desperately!

Some teenagers turn on themselves their fear, anger, and shame about their *own* real or imagined limitations. But you can't bury them—they reappear in chronic fussiness, a rash of pet peeves, or a splitting headache! A person who

learns to respect his own worth not only scorns to hit out at
others by doing mean and petty things; he also understands
that punishing himself is futile when his real problem is his
doubt of himself. He faces this problem; he sets out to learn
the skills and to develop the attitudes which will result in
his respecting himself and finding himself genuinely welcomed among his contemporaries.

Stealing, truancy, and lying are frequently results of fear.
Truancy—from work or from school—may be escape from a
situation in which failure seems ever-present; or it may be
action taken to punish adults who make too many demands.
Stealing and lying may result from the teenager's fear that
the group will exclude him if he does not have, or pretend
to have, money or clothes. Such actions, also, may be an
attempt to gain attention if a teenager fears that he is not
approved. Again, they may be indicative of a need to get
back at someone—or the world. These teenagers need to
learn that they resorted to this behavior because they were
too fearful to confront their problems directly.

Some people are so afraid to meet life alone that they
tend to lean on other people. Sometimes they idealize
others. You know the cow-eyed devotion, the unctuous
"Oh, he's wonderful!" attitude of the person generally called
a "hero worshiper." Such a person may become a carbon
copy of his hero, may substitute his hero's achievements
for his own, or may ecstatically abase himself to his hero;
for example, he may spend his days running errands for his
hero. Such a relationship can exist even in marriage.

Teenagers who, with monotonous regularity, depreciate
themselves feel safe only if they are like someone they consider desirable. Then they discover that the hero has faults!

They feel "let down." The two must part, says the immature worshiper! He suffers greatly. In *great* unhappiness, however, there is more than a little pride and hurt vanity. The sufferer is the center of everything—no one has ever suffered as he—when, in fact, everyone has known the pain of "good-by-to-it-all." The immature person forgets that, after every parting, comes a meeting with someone new. Unless he grows up, every meeting will be a new bondage. He will go through the same cycle of behavior with a new person.

An immature relationship fosters fear. True, in *every* intimate friendship between two people, there is fear: a mixture of the fear of not being understood and the terror of being understood. Everyone wants his friend to understand him in order to care about him, yet does not want his friend to see anything unbearable. A mature person resolves this conflict by reassuring himself that no one is a mirror without flaws. He can trust his friend to accept him as he is, in spite of his flaws. When one can face one's own imperfections, one no longer demands perfection in others.

Teenagers need to grow toward a "self" they can depend on so that they need not cling to anyone. It is deeply unfair to yourself and others to live someone else's life or to force someone else to live your life. Have you ever been in a household where a son or daughter "gave up" marriage to care for a parent who demanded undivided attention? Have you watched the course of a friendship between two people of the same sex who depend too much on one another for companionship?

The person who tries to live another's life becomes, first, subtly irritated at the other person, then demanding and possessive about him. After all, if one's parent or friend becomes one's entire life, one is deeply unhappy away from this person. If one devotes one's life to this person, one makes excessive demands on him or her, even becomes jealous of others with whom the "loved" person spends time! All others are rivals—therefore one must disparage them.

On the other hand, hero worship can be advantageous in a teenager's development. His heroes are his first choices of the kind of person he wishes to become. They are influential in determining which ideals he will form and for which achievements he will strive. On condition that his goals are real and possible for him if he works steadily toward them, a teenager draws strength from the examples set him; you may say he is "inspired" by his heroes to attempt to realize his ideals.

Some people avoid or escape their fears. Many people are victims of circumstances which have repeatedly threatened their self-respect. Their contacts with people have impressed them, on the whole, with their own inadequacy. They, therefore, become fearful of criticism; they dare not risk failure. Consequently, they evade responsibility; they tend to avoid situations in which they cannot be sure of success. These people may develop "escape mechanisms," such as shyness, sulkiness, unapproachability, cheating, bluffing, reforming others, daydreaming, procrastination, overdependence on others, preoccupation with details, failing to finish what they have begun, blaming others when things go wrong, drinking, illness, drugs, even mental ill-health and suicide.

Do you know a fellow who cheated in the exam? It was his way of evading what was difficult. Perhaps he did so because of pressure from his family for good grades or because he needs to meet the academic standards which will keep him in school and so postpone his entrance into the service; perhaps he holds a job or spends so much time in athletic activities that he has insufficient time for study; perhaps this is one of those required courses which he sees no point in taking; perhaps he dislikes the teacher, has failed to meet his day-by-day assignments and now wants to avoid the consequences of his neglect. There are multiple reasons for all behavior. The fact remains that the fellow failed to face an actual situation.

Nor is cheating confined to the classroom. A teenager is cheating just as surely when he fools himself into thinking that drinking will give him courage—or when she breaks a date with one boy because she's found another she likes better, and lies to the first, telling him that she is ill! The point in each life situation is: whom are you cheating? By failing to face reality, you are undermining yourself. You gain self-confidence only if you *face* life as it comes and take responsibility for situations you created.

Some teenagers rely on excuses to explain mistakes and failures; they blame other people or their past for their disappointments and their want of success in developing their possibilities. One may say, "If the umpire had been fair, we'd have won that game." Another may moan that, because her family hasn't enough money or she is not pretty, she can't hope to be popular, to become editor of the school paper, to make the Sub-Deb Club or that junior executive position.

This is called "projection": the person is projecting the blame for his or her inadequacy onto someone else. He may sense, dimly, that *he* might have had some responsibility in a situation; but he is afraid to admit his mistakes, his limitations or someone's displeasure with him. Everyone sometimes blames other people—or the situation! But if a person does so too often, he needs not sympathy but a mirror. When things always go wrong, take a good long look at yourself!

Relying on excuses can paralyze one in the present. You know the kind of person who does no more than bewail his fate and hope for "a better break" in the future, yet turns down opportunities which may lead to that break? Suppose a teenager was asked today to try out for the swimming squad or the track team or to write a story for the school paper. Did he seize these opportunities or did he invent elaborate excuses why he could not do so? No matter how insecure a person's past may have made him, flimsy excuses do not explain today's failures and inaction. Such a person would understand his problems more clearly if he intelligently confronted "how he got that way." Everyone can *learn* from his past—if he does not merely suffer because of it or place the blame for all present ills on it!

Hoping for a better future can be wise. A teenager can bring into the present some of the joy and excitement of future success by anticipating it *if* through dreams of the future he is energized to decision, action, assumption of his day-by-day responsibilities. However, some people cannot resist the temptation to dream rather than to act—especially if they doubt their own power to carry out responsibilities or to make "right" decisions!

It is easy to resent your limitations and to daydream about what you'd do if you were someone else—or had another's chance! Suppose a teenager is unhappy because he is not popular with the opposite sex? How comfortable to picture oneself happily married, the master or mistress of a beautiful home! But what is that person doing today to learn to get along with the opposite sex?

Daydreams can be a preview of a glorious future or they can be an "easy way out." One teenager is bursting with ideas, visualizing a future with much adventure and many achievements—and is planning how to *realize* these possibilities. Another teenager, disappointed in himself or fearful lest people important to him are dissatisfied with him, becomes, in his imagination, whatever he thinks will make "them" pay attention to him. Such teenagers may see themselves as the five-letter man in athletics, the best-dressed girl on campus, the most "up and coming" young executive in the city, the most popular "date" in the sorority, a Metropolitan Opera star! However, dreams alone are futile.

If someone wants to be a four-letter man, then he must go out every day—and weekends—for practice regardless of what tempting alternatives the family or the gang offer; he must refrain from smoking; be in bed early, even after a heavy date for the big dance! The girl who would be the "best-dressed" must study costume design, color, and fabric, must learn to buy wisely or sew well. The aspiring executive may need to go to night school; he must gain the requisite knowledge, skills, and work habits to become recognized as someone with a genuine contribution to make to his employer. If a teenager would be popular, he or she must learn to meet people easily, be interested in them, talk well, enjoy parties, and develop a variety of skills such as dancing, tennis, swimming, skiing, skating.

The would-be opera star, on the other hand, must be willing to give up a social life and spend hours learning libretti, voice, acting, dancing, languages. Read the life story of Kirsten Flagstad, the great Wagnerian soprano, formerly of the Metropolitan Opera, if you tend to dream only about the glamor of such a future. You need to find out about the heartbreak too, and to train yourself, without flinching, to face the fact that all learning inevitably involves immense effort, many failures, frequent awkwardness, some social breaks and some sour notes.

When some teenagers are unhappy in a group, when they feel inadequate, or when someone has hurt their feelings, they become shy and they withdraw from action. Shyness may take the form of refusal to meet new people or to try a new skill, of getting off in the corner and reading a book, or of disappearing entirely. These unhappy people may also weep, stamp their feet, or snivel in self-pity about how useless they are; they may bitterly assert that "It's no use trying! I can't do anything right!" Perhaps they hope to avoid rejection by "not getting involved" with people, reasoning that if they say nothing, they will offend no one; if they do nothing, no one will discover their limitations. No one will discover them at all! Shyness and emotional outbursts cover fear—but we're all scared about trying something new! There has to be a first time for everyone.

All this behavior originates in some painful experience. Everyone goes through unhappy times; however, *because* of them, one may learn some truth about oneself or gain a greater understanding of other people.

Some teenagers hope to protect themselves from facing their fears and anxiety by thinking up good explanations

66

for their behavior. Have you seen teenagers become exceptionally polite, neat, precise, careful, or preoccupied with details? It is as though they were saying to themselves, "I have failed—or I have not been loved—because I was bad or careless. If I am careful and orderly, if I do the right thing, then people may like me." Everyone uses the technique sometimes. Haven't you found yourself thinking up *good* reasons for something you did—when you knew these weren't the *real* reasons?

Since our society places so much stress on being "reasonable" and "logical," unhappy people overuse this method of evading their problems. Such people need help in facing the truth about themselves and in meeting their real problems in a constructive manner. Just telling other people what a mess you are doesn't absolve you from doing something about it!

Some teenagers attempt to escape their worries in overactivity and "socialization." The teenager who, too obviously, rushes around being in every school, campus, or community activity or being "the life" of every party may do so because he is afraid that people will think he is unpopular if he is not always "on the go." Perhaps he does not want to be alone because he is not comfortable with himself. All teenagers like friends and fun; but mature teenagers are selective about their friends. They also like some quiet time to themselves—a little privacy now and then!

What of teenagers who have so many irons in the fire, yet who always promise to do more? Those who boast of their activities or who move constantly from one activity to another may be fearful that they cannot "deliver"—

that they will not make good their promises. They become tense and irritable if someone tries to hold them to *one* assigned task. They prefer to believe that they did not do something because they had too much to do; it is too humiliating to face the fact that they may not have known how to do what they promised or that they did not plan their time well and assumed responsibility for more than they could do!

Have you known someone who begins a project with fanfare but seldom carries through? Perhaps such a person leaves tasks unfinished rather than submit his work to others' appraisal! He may be unable to admit that he makes mistakes; he may be unable to bear criticism. Therefore he avoids—or, at least, postpones—appraisal of his work by not finishing it. Thus he can always excuse himself with "If I'd had time to finish it, things would have been different." Such "rationalization" hides feelings of inadequacy and resultant fears of failure.

Most teenagers need help in budgeting time so as to include participation in as many activities as possible. However, they also need to learn to say "no" without feeling threatened. If a teenager takes on more responsibilities than he can carry or promises to do something which he has neither time nor skill to do creditably, he inevitably faces failure and the necessity for excusing or explaining it.

Nor does any teenager want to become unapproachable. People with a "better-than-thou" attitude are actually the victims of a paralyzing cynicism in relation to themselves. They hide genuine fear behind a gruff manner and bitter words. They are unhappy individuals who remain aloof because they are afraid to meet people lest others discover their inadequacies—real or imagined.

Jealousy, too, is related to a feeling of inadequacy. A teenager may be jealous of the person who has something he wants or is something he wants to be. Jealousy *can*, on the other hand, be one's motivation in striving for what one wants—a more attractive physical appearance, a better job, a boy or girl friend. Depending on the use made of it, jealousy can be the basis for acceptable or unacceptable behavior.

Jealousy can spur teenagers on toward doing their best work, putting their "best foot forward." It need not be confined to destructive behavior, such as trying to undermine another's reputation because one feels unable to compete honestly with him.

Occasionally people hope to escape responsibility—or the anxiety of facing their own inadequacy—by illness. Doctors have emphasized, in recent years, that some illnesses are related to certain feelings. For example, a person's fear of his unrestrained hates, angers, or loves may result in headaches, nervous conditions, digestive upsets, stomach ulcers, high blood pressure.

Many times, fear aroused by feelings of inadequacy, of disapproval or rejection, may be translated into physical symptoms: in other words, a person may build up resentments which he thinks he dare not express, even to himself, lest he lose more of his self-respect; he thinks he dare not confide in other people lest he progressively lose their love and respect. By shutting in these feelings or trying to ignore them, such a person is literally turning them on himself and suffering physical pain rather than the mental anguish of thinking himself unwanted and inadequate. If your "self" is sick, your body cannot be well.

Accidents may also be related to anxiety. When people are afraid that they cannot perform their tasks skilfully and well, they are tense and thus more likely to do poorly than if they had more confidence in themselves.

Some people seem to have more "accidents" than others. They may be people who are generally awkward, fearful, lacking in skill or self-confidence. Again, they may be individuals whose minds are on their worries rather than on what they are doing at the moment.

Since the purpose of an escape mechanism is to keep a person from feeling his fear and anxiety, this interchange of feelings goes on unconsciously, beyond the limits of awareness. A person *thinks* that he is really ill or that he is just unlucky enough to have an accident. Illness in any form can become a powerful weapon; it looks real and its results are effective. No one expects a sick or injured person to do anything difficult or to make any momentous decisions. He can even "get back" at people who rejected him by forcing them to take care of him! It also gives him something concrete and "respectable" to worry about. However, an illness or an accident cannot help you to escape your "self" and its problems; it merely forces your anxieties and fears temporarily into a different channel.

Most teenagers dare not—or think they dare not—say, "I'm so afraid that my anxiety has made me ill." Yet all of us know that our feelings and our bodies interact. Haven't you felt your knees wobble or your stomach turn over because you had to take an examination or act in a play? Your body is not something separate from your "self."

On the contrary, your body may possess wisdom which your "self" needs to assimilate. Your bodily reactions warn you that your "self" is "up against it." If you sidetrack the warning into exclusive concern with your physical condition, if, when you actually are ill, you "give yourself over to misery"—neither your body nor your "self" can get well. Try using your illness to become acquainted with your "self" —face and resolve the emotions which harass you!

Most teenagers need to learn to use their bodies more effectively. What must you find out about the way *your* body works if you are to live at your maximum-efficiency level? Do you know, for example, how many hours of sleep *you* need? Some people actually need only five or six, others —throughout their lives—need ten if they are to be at their best. At what time of day can *you* expect to produce your best work? Some people rise early, bound out of bed, shower and exercise zestfully, attack the day's work vigorously, but go into a slump at about four o'clock in the afternoon. Others hate to get up, grope and grouch when the alarm rings, need coffee poured into them before they are decent to live with, build up their energy slowly, are "going great guns" in the late afternoon and often do their best work at night. It's a matter of blood pressure, habit, and temperament, doctors say!

What of exercise and relaxation? Do you know how to "let down" from strain? What works with you—a brisk walk, a game of tennis, a warm bath, hot milk, looking at the stars, or a detective story? Have you learned also to relax by varying work as well as by exchanging work for recreation?

Another method by which teenagers seek to evade facing their anxiety and fear of inadequacy is bluffing. It looks successful; but he who bluffs finds it difficult to live up to the pose he created! Usually, he cannot do what he extravagantly claimed to be able to do; he is not what he professed to be; he does not possess what he said he had nor believe what he said he did. Moreover, he cannot concentrate on developing his real "self" because he created a phony one. Such a teenager would be freer if he could admit his limitations and concentrate on developing his real abilities—rather than living in fear of having his bluff called!

None of us can be all that we want to be or have all that we want to have physically, materially, socially. Therefore, every mature person substitutes what he can for what he cannot have. The above paragraphs are not to be construed to mean that compensation is unwise. Some of the world's best-known people compensated for some shortcoming: Franklin Delano Roosevelt could not even walk alone; Helen Keller is blind and deaf; Alec Templeton's monologues on the piano are so famous that few people think of him as a blind man. These people consciously set out to compensate for their limitations—and succeeded brilliantly. You can too! You need not resort to second-rate behavior.

There are also leaners—people continuously begging for advice or wanting others to make their decisions. Unfortunately, some adults encourage teenagers in such behavior; they are flattered by being asked to dictate to teenagers. Some adults praise overcompliance, blind obedience, and conformity—not realizing that, if they really wanted to help these teenagers, they would guide them into situations where, gradually, the leaners could develop courage to make their own decisions, accept responsibility for their own choices, and develop their own potentialities.

Teenagers who won't make up their own minds also are insecure. They *say* that they want someone to decide for them; but, if someone does, they blame this person when things go wrong. Another technique for avoiding choices is to delay a choice so long that one can say that something "just happened."

Everyone who refuses to make his own choice actually is afraid that he may make a wrong choice. However, we all live in a world where choice is inevitable. One can continue drifting only at a price—living constantly with uncertainty and inner conflict! As a person is confronted by one situation after another in which choice is necessary, he becomes progressively less able to concentrate on anything except "What shall I do?" His emotions are dissipated; he keeps wondering what might happen if he followed this course— or that! Who would deny himself the peace of mind decision will bring?

Some teenagers "procrastinate"—and who doesn't? If a difficult, unpleasant task faces you, you postpone it. Perhaps you dissipate your energies by concentrating on details. You do errands, shine your shoes, manicure your nails, clean out your bureau drawers, and brush the dog to distract yourself and others from the fact that you feel unable or unwilling to face the real task—whether it is mowing the lawn, doing the ironing, or studying for an examination. What is your version of "get going"? Say it quick!

Other teenagers "forget" incidents which involved humiliation or embarrassment. No one likes to remember the unpleasant; in fact, when we have learned all we can from an unhappy experience, it is better to forget it than to brood over it. On the other hand, if people have been deeply hurt by an experience, some haven't the courage to face it. They *bury* it in the hope of forgetting it. Psychologists say that they are "repressing" their feelings. Feelings, however, do not stay buried—or repressed—or forgotten; they haunt a person until he gathers courage to face and resolve them.

Habitual gambling is another escape from life's responsibilities. Certainly, everyone gambles sometimes; it is fun to try to win a contest, a game of chance, or an athletic meet. One gambles on a "bargain"; there is great satisfaction in getting something without having to pay full price. However, life seldom gives something for nothing.

We have discussed many ways in which people avoid facing anything painful. Alcohol may also be used to escape reality. Suppose an adult has had a "hard day"—he has lived through a series of unpleasant incidents. He goes out to dinner and wants to forget his worries. "Taking a drink" often begins in a social situation like this. He does forget his troubles—temporarily; but drinking does not *resolve* difficulties. This is done only as a person courageously faces each problem and learns to understand its significance.

Some teenagers resort to drugs to dull life's pain—whether the pain be an aching tooth or pain deep inside because no one cares. Other teenagers hope, through drugs, to escape life's problems. Still others, unconsciously, want to destroy themselves. Using drugs is a legal offense; therefore, the unhappy teenager may also derive satisfaction rebelling against society. But his perception is faulty. Most legal restrictions protect the group from the rebellious individual; for example, to protect property, laws are made against stealing.

The law against drugs protects the *individual*. The individual who breaks this law hurts only himself. An analogy is the law that people be vaccinated against smallpox. The individual who defies it will be ill. If a teenager exposes himself to drug addiction, he will become dangerously ill. He will, in addition, find himself a parasite on society, unemployed and unemployable.

People who consider themselves failures may be driven to the depths of despair—sometimes even to suicide or mental illness. National studies emphasize that probably ten per cent of our country's people will spend some time in a mental hospital because they have lost touch with reality in attempting to escape anxiety about themselves. If these people are to be cured, they must be helped to face life—to take both approval and disapproval, success and failure. For such people, an important part of the cure is to discover that they are not as contemptible and ineffective as they thought they were—and that there are people who care about them.

We All Have Feelings

Because we are human, we have all kinds of feelings—good and bad. The mature person readily admits that sometimes he is in the heights, sometimes in the depths. Sometimes he is sad and unhappy; sometimes he is mad at his friends or family; sometimes he is afraid—or happy—or bored—or lonely—or tired. As he expresses his feelings, possibly he finds himself resorting to the second-rate behavior described in this chapter. Not a living person can honestly say that he has not occasionally behaved in some of these ways!

However, the mature person recognizes *when* he is behaving so; he tries to understand *why* and resolutely faces himself with, "It's your life! Take charge! Find a better way to handle those feelings!" Feelings need to be recognized and accepted. Only when you understand how you feel can you steer and control feeling. Some channels for expressing feelings are sanctioned; some are not. You need to say, "Certainly, I feel that way. This way of getting it out is permissible. That way is not." Thus you differentiate between feelings and actions.

The mature person is not afraid of his feelings; he does not feel compelled to deny them or snuff them out. A mature "self" is free to face the full impact of fear, for who is not afraid when there is occasion to be frightened? A mature "self" is able to recognize the depths of anger and hate, for who has not felt them in certain situations? A mature "self" can thrill to success, joy, tenderness and compassion, for who does not possess capacity to enjoy, to laugh, and to love?

On the other hand, a mature person knows that anyone who expresses feelings indiscriminately may hurt himself and others—like the adult "spoiled brat" who "explodes" when he doesn't get what he wants. Or he may sound insincere, as does any person who "emotes" all the time.

Yet, if a person never expresses his hates, angers, loves, and fears, these "bottle up" inside him and he goes around afraid to say anything lest he "lose control" and say too much. People who habitually "hold in" and repress strong feelings often find themselves "pushed around" by those feelings—driven into unrestrained behavior so different from their usual way of acting that it completely mystifies them. Such behavior was discussed in this chapter.

Controlling feelings does not mean pretending they do not exist. Control means expressing feelings in a way that fits the situation. The problem is to express positive and negative feelings, impulses, and needs legitimately in ways that will not hurt yourself or others. For example, you may channel feelings into action that discharges tension but harms no one—such as talking, painting, woodworking, or strenuous exercise. You may transform feelings into thoughts, so that you are not swayed by your moods. You may demonstrate that you believe so firmly in the feelings you express that you will take responsibility for decisions based on them. The person who cannot express feelings seems cold. To the degree that you can learn to handle your feelings maturely, you deepen your understanding of and sympathy with others as they struggle with their feelings.

You've Got What It Takes

"KNOW THYSELF" is a challenge. You will be started on the longest journey you've ever made if, step by step, you try to go back through your life and the lives of those nearest you to find the places where things "took a wrong turn." You will face embarrassing experiences, painful, even bitter

78

ones which you would prefer to forget. It is humiliating to look at the fact that *you* were ever "like that."

You don't "forget" difficult experiences, you merely shove them from consciousness. But they persist because they have hurt and because they are associated with anxiety and danger. Dick's story in Chapter One illustrates how this might happen. Dick thought his parents' love was unequally divided. He felt that he could not compete with his sister. He hated school because it represented failure to compete: academically and physically he felt small and weak. The day came when he couldn't "take it" any more; he "let go"—not deliberately, of course. Yet he felt guilty because he knew how angry he was inside. What he really felt guilty about was that he hated his sister and his parents and wanted to hurt somebody.

Yes, Dick has plenty of trouble. No matter what he does, he never seems to do the right thing! Everybody thinks he's a "no-good," he says. Dick could have kept on feeling sorry for himself—or worrying other folks! But Dick chose to learn from his trouble.

Dick got his *real* problem out where he could look at it— his guilt about hating, his fear of inadequacy in competing. One can't get the good out of a painful experience by hiding it and running away from the memory. One must, as it were, take it in one's hands and squeeze down until one has gotten all the good out. Then the rest can't hurt any more.

Dick is learning to put his troubles into words. He is facing the fact that his manner of dealing with his troubles was poor. When he can re-think all that he did—summon all the details at will to consider the significance of his actions—then, although he will admit that he made a mistake, he will be using the mistake as a learning experience. As though he were saying, "I was wrong there, but now I know better ways to help myself."

Everyone Can Learn to Change

Everyone has opportunities to learn this method of dealing with his daily experiences. Each of us has left behind us, in our lives, a trail of thoughts, acts, and feelings of which we are profoundly ashamed. We've also had experiences which have so terrified us that we've said unconsciously, "I'll never do *that* again"—and "that" may refer to something as basic as trusting someone, giving someone unqualified affection, making decisions for ourselves—or to something as comparatively unimportant as trying to swim, play tennis, or be a brilliant conversationalist.

How might a person handle his "trouble"? He might be haunted by things he did which frightened or shamed him. He may remember only that when he tried "that" before someone ridiculed him, made a fool of him, or told him he'd "never learn," he was just too dumb or awkward or unattractive. He might talk back to people who ridicule him. Nevertheless, his actions show that he believes them—he avoids situations in which certain behavior is necessary, then feels inadequate because he cannot do these things.

That a person *does* not do things does not mean he *can* not. If he is willing to look at the reasons *why* he is not doing them, he may find that he's never really tried—after the first time! He was easily dissuaded! After all, who learns to play tennis without making a fool of himself on the court many times; who becomes the "life of the party" without trying out some jokes poorly before he learns to make a joke go over? And as for loving and trusting people, it may be well to learn early in life that not everyone knows how to accept love and trust. Some people *may* let you down. Do you, therefore, want to become suspicious and cynical about everyone? *You can learn to love and to trust only by loving and trusting.* Try again—there are many warm, gentle, and loyal people in this world!

Everyone needs to learn to accept variations in his behavior without criticizing himself harshly or despairing of himself. Does he make allowances for himself or is he expecting too much of himself—too much independence, too much freedom from fear, guilt, hostility—possibly too perfect an adjustment in his family, with his friends or the opposite sex? We all have "bad" days, especially when some minor or major crisis has caused us to "revert" to behavior we might otherwise deplore. Do not condemn yourself too hastily!

Suppose a mature person feels gripped by the old shame and terror as he "tries again" to face a painful experience? He doesn't pretend that shame or terror isn't there. It possessed *all* of him once; it paralyzed him into inaction. Some of it will be with him the rest of his life. He accepts this fact. He looks shame or terror in the face; he learns to live with it.

He accepts the fact that everyone has characteristics that might be called negative. We all hate ourselves sometimes for some stupidity; we're all afraid sometimes. Everyone occasionally dislikes his family or detests his teacher or employer! Now and then everyone uses poor judgment in the way he displays fear and anger! After all, anyone who was perfect would find it difficult to live in an unfinished world.

It will take time to learn this process of considering, reconsidering, and digesting the meaning of one's daily experiences. As a person becomes increasingly able to ask "Why do *I* need to behave this way?" and to take responsibility for his *own* behavior, he frees himself to control the present. His past no longer controls him. He is not bound by self-absorption or self-distrust.

He looks to his past for explanations of his behavior; he builds on this knowledge. Gradually, he learns to use his emotions constructively; less frequently does he limit his expression of them to futile regrets or rebellion against his "environment" or his limitations. Less often does he need to blame others for *his* mistakes and shortcomings. No longer does he fear his emotions; he knows that both the pain and the joy he gives—and must take—are the price everyone pays who becomes involved in life.

Thus a person can learn, day by day, to do a fair, realistic job of handling his problems. If he finds strength to continue to face his real self and respect what he sees, then, in spite of his mistakes, his shortcomings, his fears and doubts, he will become an individual who can depend on himself. He will have earned his *self*-confidence.

Many teenagers need to be left alone to work out their problems. They need to keep their troubles to themselves—to be trusted to find their own way! For some teenagers, it is very difficult to talk to anyone about themselves, especially to adults. However, not everyone can, unaided, find strength to handle his problems. Most of us need to have other people reach toward us, be patient with our fears and inadequacies, our failures and mistakes, understand our need to love and our need to hate, yet stand by and help us as we try to change.

82

Dr. Karl Menninger, an eminent psychiatrist, emphasizes this need for the give-and-take of warm affection in human relationships when he says, "You can live if you can love." In the warmth of other people's steady affection for you, of their unwavering belief in you as you are, you can cease condemning yourself for what you are not. You slowly gain courage to take a good long look at yourself—to see why you have accumulated *your particular* fears and inadequacies. Finally, you are able to seek out and take advantage of new experiences which will wipe out unhappy memories, doubts, and fears.

If most teenagers cannot take this "long look" at themselves entirely alone; if they need sympathetic friends with whom they can talk about their problems and hopes, how much more do teenagers who have had experiences involving painful emotional upsets need help! Once started on this "longest journey," they must relive these unhappy experiences by relating to an understanding person all the details connected with them so that they see their real significance and thus release the emotion around them. The person who helps effect this release should be a trained counselor or a psychiatrist—a person especially skilled in handling personality problems. Such people are to be found in increasing numbers in counseling centers or in guidance or mental health clinics in schools, colleges, industries, hospitals, and communities.

Why Some People Resist Change

The really tragic person is one who never attempts the journey. He cannot reach out toward people because he is absorbed with himself. Why does he remain "self-centered"?

If someone's life has been so difficult or so easy, if he has
been so hurt, neglected, and rejected, or so over-protected
and indulged that he, as an individual, never mattered much
—then that person may spend the rest of his life trying to
prove to himself that he *does* matter, that what *he* wants
and needs is important. Yet, he doesn't quite believe it, perhaps because important people early in his life did not believe it. If he did believe it, he would not be so absorbed
in proving it.

When someone feels that he himself is not very important,
obviously he cannot believe that other people matter. So
he goes in circles, acting as though only he himself mattered,
yet not daring to look at himself because he is afraid perhaps he doesn't. He cannot risk facing the fact that he really
was not very important to people who should have—according to accepted standards—loved him, people like his parents. He thinks, miserably, perhaps he is not very deserving
of love!

Unfortunately, some children have been deeply hurt by
their early experiences. If such was *your* lot, you may face
it, drain out the bitterness and reach for help in building a
"self"—or you may go on pretending that life really wasn't
like that! Some people pretend. They never look back.
Some look around them to manipulate other people and continue the illusion of their own self-importance.

As long as you see other people only as agents to bolster
your ego, you cannot establish affectionate give-and-take relationships. A self-centered person cannot *share* thoughts
and feelings. He can give and he can take; but his idea of
giving is flattery—he "makes friends" with people who have
84

what he wants—glamor, social ease, sophistication, money
or "importance." He lets it be known that they are his
"friends." He can *take* from others; in fact, his "friends"
will uncritically bestow on him any amount of flattery—
will tell him continuously how wonderful he is. "Friends"
are often people in whom he is "interested," to whom he is
being "kind" or for whom he is doing favors—so that he
can feel superior and "necessary"!

Adult friendship he cannot bear. It would be too painful
for him to know that his friends see him for what he is; he
could not believe that they would love him anyway. Con-
versely, he cannot see people for what *they* are and love
them anyway because that would destroy his picture of
what he thinks they are—important, glamorous, sophisti-
cated.

A person may remain self-centered all his life—even
though he or she becomes a wife or husband, a successful
lawyer, business man or woman, doctor, or professor. People may use their families, their colleagues, their job itself
to build up this illusion of their own importance. Often,
people like this are very gregarious. They love "social contacts"! They may be brilliant conversationalists, sought
after for parties. However, there is urgency about their so-
cializing. They "like their friends around" them because
they "cannot bear" to be alone. They don't really like themselves.

Should their "friends" turn to such people in a crisis, they
would find that these people can't feel. They've taught
themselves not to: it's as though they had said, "I've been
hurt and hurt so much that I'll never feel again." This is

the reason why they let their "friends" down—they don't know what caring about anyone means! Their emotions are confined to superficial demonstrations of affection and outbursts of temper when they are blocked in something they want to do. But to feel deeply, to care enough about another person to be able to put themselves in his place and understand his pain and need—this they have never dared do.

Perhaps they could learn—if they could see themselves as they are and admit that they need help. But people like this seldom see themselves as they really are. They have for so long considered themselves adequate, successful! Their "friends" have reinforced this illusion—and other people seldom "tell them off." Thus they actually do not know what they look like to an unprejudiced person.

To people like this, seeking help would seem a token of weakness. In reality, accepting help would be a frightening experience. It would mean that change in themselves was necessary. Such people have felt compelled to avoid changing themselves. Consequently, it would take a situation involving personal pride—threat of a divorce or losing a job—before they would even entertain the proposition that the only way to escape preoccupation with oneself is, gradually, to develop sufficient self-liking and self-trust to turn one's attention away from oneself to other people and the outer world of reality.

No one can help people until they want to be helped. And insecure people often resist help. It bespeaks courage, never weakness, to seek help, to be willing to relinquish habits which give you many satisfactions, to admit that you do not know all the answers, to trust yourself to another and to face the fact that you might be a happier, more effective, or pleasanter person for your friends, coworkers, and family to live with!

Give Yourself a Chance!

So you have discovered that you need not remain as you are, that human beings possess the unique characteristic of being able to change! Because we can stand outside the present and imagine ourselves in the past or in the future, we can learn from the past and prepare for the future. Everyone uses this technique of looking "before and after": remember how you anticipated and prepared for your first date, how you regretted a social error or stupid remark?

Your progress toward a "new self" depends on how you relate to every day's experiences: Are you pretending to be something you are not? Are you being only what "is expected"? Are you being yourself defiantly—the "I'll show them" kind of person? Or are you learning to decide and to do in your daily life not what you believe will gain you praise but what you believe is honest and true to yourself? Are you facing the fact that you have limitations in equipment and past experience which will make it impossible for you to do and be all that you *will* to do or try to be? Can you confront yourself *as you are*, learn from what you see and make the most of it according to your lights? Do you look at what you want to be and do, then at what you are and can do—and work to bring your expectations to reality?

Growing daily in understanding and control of your behavior, you experience the satisfaction of knowing that your past problems no longer halt your growth or limit your activities. Your self-respect increases because you are conquering your fear that you aren't adequate or aren't like someone else. As you successfully do things you were formerly afraid to do, faith in yourself develops out of the death throes of fear. You learn to believe in yourself because you find that you can confront anxiety, answer it with courage, live with it, or overcome it constructively.

To paraphrase an eminent psychiatrist: Given a chance, you tend to develop your *particular* human potentialities, the *unique* alive forces of your real self; the faculty to express yourself and relate yourself to others with your *spontaneous* feelings; the ability to tap your *own* resources, capacities, and gifts. This will in time enable you to find *your* set of values and aims in life. Thus, you grow toward "self-realization." You *know* you are your "self."

Living Begins at Home

MANY TEENAGERS say that their parents do not understand them. Often, they are right! Many parents say that their offspring do not understand them. And they are often right!

Who Understands Whom?

When teenagers say that their parents do not understand them, they generally mean either that they do not understand why their parents make the demands they do or that they do not trust their parents—in the sense that they do not confide in them. On the other hand, teenagers—even those who have had an ideal childhood—may be very difficult for parents to understand during the years when they are trying to achieve the feeling of being persons in their own right. Growing up sometimes may be a time of explosive emotional outbursts—or of emotional withdrawal from parents. You find yourself pulling away from your parents, not because of lack of love for them, but because you are annoyed by a sense of dependence in yourself; this reminds you that with the body and appearance of a mature person, you have only the experience of youth.

You must blend all you have learned by identification and contact with others—then come up with a personality of your own! The most that parents can do for growing young people is to believe in them and wait, bearing in mind that their relationships at this time are complicated, yet delicately balanced, and that social and emotional factors outside the home are influencing them profoundly. The kind of people one's parents are, is important; but teenagers are taking the easy way out if, when they don't like what they are making of themselves, they blame their parents. One teenager realistically faces her responsibility as she writes in her diary: "How true Daddy's words were. 'All children must look after their own upbringing.' Parents can only give good advice and put them on the right paths, but the final forming of a person's character lies in his own hands." *

However, parents worry about your future. Some even torture themselves into thinking that they determine your

* Anne Frank, *The Diary of a Young Girl,* Doubleday & Company, Inc., New York, 1952, p. 275.

90

future. Parents are also people. They may be puzzled, happy, sad, uncertain people. Most of them are very eager to be friends with their children. Sometimes they become discouraged and self-critical because teenagers "always want to get out of the house. Perhaps we haven't been good parents to them." Sometimes they feel that they have given teenagers every ounce of love and consideration, yet "youth is ungrateful."

Especially if a teenager is a first or an only child and his parents are unaccustomed to teenagers, they may be unprepared for some of your behavior. For example, they may misunderstand your negative feelings toward them. They may regard them as personal affronts or may consider withdrawal as loss of love. As a result, the relationship between parents and teenagers now and then can become acutely unhappy.

Little by little, your parents are trying, not only to face, but to accept the fact that they are not as important to you as they once were. It is most difficult to relinquish the feeling of being needed and the pleasure of caring for a helpless child. Painfully, parents must now learn to derive pleasure from the increasing ability of a growing individual to think and act independently from them. It takes courage to allow independence; for example, to encourage a teenager to learn a skill in which the results may be tragic—and permanent—such as riding his or her bicycle in traffic, playing on the football team, driving a car, or piloting a plane.

It takes flexibility and open-mindedness for parents to substitute reasoning for authority. Sometimes parents from habit give an order and expect it to be carried out; it seems a much easier and quicker way of getting things done than to discuss the situation with the teenager. Moreover, after discussion, a parent might, sometimes, have to decide that the order was not necessary after all! It is difficult for all of us to admit a mistake; it is particularly disheartening to parents who may have felt for years that to protect their children they must be always right.

When you justly resent too many orders or too much pressure for unquestioning obedience, do you also realize that, often, these demands result from your parents' honest fear that harm may come to you? Parents are especially fearful when they wonder whether they have overprotected you and are doubtful whether you have learned to protect yourself!

As your parents sense your resentment of their protection, they become apprehensive lest they lose you. Such apprehension is especially strong in parents who do not understand that young people desire their care and direction, but want different methods used in imparting it. This is an elusive distinction. The fact remains that your parents will require assurance that you can take care of yourself before they will renounce responsibility for you. These feelings explain some of the "mistakes" which, you may feel, your parents make in their relationship with you. Though they are adults, they have not reached "perfection"! Nor will you!

If both you and your parents can recognize that, in spite of everything, you still want and need each other in a different way from childhood, you can help one another to lessen the hurt as you grow toward independence. You can all learn to discuss, without bitterness, the strain you are under as you try to assert yourself in order to stop being a baby and to begin being an individual in the family.

If you can find within yourself patience gradually to work out with your parents your changing role, you and they will develop confidence in one another. As a result, you can, without too many fears and too much guilt, move ahead in self-development to stand at last as an individual in the world outside your home. Most parents fervently desire the mutual respect and trust resulting from this joint effort. They are eager to help you learn to develop independence from them because they know that by being willing to give you up they earn your love and friendship.

You Want Independence

Gaining independence, like becoming a person, is a long process. Originally, the child was an organic unit with his mother. Physically, he became an individual at birth. His consciousness of "self" probably had its rudimentary beginnings when the infant asserted himself and screamed "I want." The child was tied to his family because it was the only world he knew in the sense of having learned to adjust to its demands in order to get what he wanted or needed.

As he moved from home to school, increasingly he had to "stand on his own feet"; he had to learn to be "free" because it was physically impossible for his parents to accompany him everywhere he went. Gradually, he had to learn to feel, to want, to experience, and to choose "on his own." As he began to mature physically, there was increasing conflict between the part of him which sought growth and independence and the part which longed to remain immature and to receive protection from adults.

Everyone's growth proceeds from the infant's innocence of any need to care for himself through the struggle of the child for and against independence, on toward genuine consciousness of one's "self" as an individual separate from others but free to relate to others. A person earns his individuality by conscious and responsible choices toward freedom and willingness to live his own life, rather than by choices toward overdependence, letting *others* make his decisions or take responsibility for what he does. Finally, a truly independent individual is able to create a new relationship to people and to the world, one of *self-chosen* love, family responsibility, creative work, and leisure.

What Is Freedom?

The central aspect of one's growth toward independence is the desire for unrestricted liberty accompanied by its opposite, a dread of the consequences of liberty. Everyone needs to accept this struggle in himself and to recognize that it can produce both good or ill, depending upon attitudes one develops toward authority. Attitudes like rebellion, submission, or blind loyalty mask contempt, even hatred. Some teenagers conceive of "authority" solely as a restraining force which would strangle their growth and rob them of power to use their potentialities. True, authority can be restrictive. When instant obedience is demanded "and no questions asked" or when punishment follows an attempt at discussion of some arbitrary command—the old "yes sir, no sir, ulcer technique"—then hatred is generated in the person forced to give up his right to exist as a human being independent of the authority, whether this be parent, teacher, employer—or government dictator. A person may seem to surrender or adjust; but actually he hates his conqueror.

Hating does serve the purpose of preserving for the per-

son some sense of strength. Thus it is better than surrender
—when a person gives up the struggle and abdicates his
"self." However, teenagers should understand why they
need to hate and what they are really hating. Actually, they
hate, not "authorities," but the demands and restrictions.

Face and resolve this hatred. Should you want *to be
against* certain demands and restrictions, keep your attention fixed on them. Know what you *are against* and why.
Have you examined the ideas against which *you* are rebelling? You may merely be tired of being told to do or
not to do so many things that you wish only to do the opposite of what you are told.

Or perhaps you gain a *delusion* of freedom by rebelling
against whatever your parents or other authorities stand
for? Have you ever pondered the fact that there must be
standards to rebel *against* or you would have no point of
reference for building different standards? Moreover, knowing only what you refuse to believe or live up to gives no
conviction or strength. This comes when you take the next
step and seek answers to: what do I want to be free *for?*
What *will* I live up to and believe? If you are fighting for
your right to be a free, responsible person, rebellion is not
enough. It is only a first step.

Freedom is a process. Rebellion is easy; you may achieve
a certain sense of power from attacking existing standards
and regulations. You may even be misled by the deception
that becoming "free" is a matter of one exciting and dramatic
blowup with your parents.

Talking loudly about wanting independence some teenagers hope will cover up the fact that they are *afraid* to
move from the protection of dependence to the "aloneness"

95

of independence. It *is* frightening to assume responsibility for your own decisions, errors, loves, hates, fears, and anxieties. However, unless you daily choose what *you* will live by, you will tend to "run back to mother." You will be tied to your home because you are afraid to face life alone.

In our society, some people think that values—even the future itself—is so uncertain that they can gain little support—or "mothering"—from believing in *their* future or being certain of definite values. It is not surprising that such insecure people tend to cling to the physical mother of their childhood who symbolizes all the security they think they will ever know. This relationship is not "love" of mother! Genuine love implies reaching out toward people. Dependency excludes "loving" all but the one person—or situation—desperately needed.

A state of dependence is not confined to family ties; you may also be abjectly dependent on prestige, public opinion, or relationships with other people. You know the kind of person who hysterically cries that "if you don't love me," or "if I don't get that promotion" or "if I don't win the election, I might as well die." Many people, if they must renounce something they want, retreat into themselves; they do "just die" with a part of themselves. These are not free people.

What should die is your attitude of dependence. If the part of you which clings frantically to this need to be loved by a certain person, to the need for prestige and public recognition *can* die, something new will be born; a stronger self, more "alive" because "you" consciously chose not to die; more secure because not tied to someone else or to fickle standards of public opinion; more joyful because "you" are fulfilling your potentialities and building your integrity.

96

This is freedom; "you" are affirming your responsibility for yourself!

Freedom is achieved gradually. Obviously, you do not automatically become "free" at a certain age. Freedom must be achieved. You will not automatically remain free; you must choose freedom each day in the decisions you make. Continuously, *you* must decide what "you" will do. Unless you so choose, you will do what others expect.

Freedom is not just saying "yes" or "no" a few times in specific situations; it is power to make choices—actually, power to mold your life. In this sense, freedom is cumulative; one choice made with some freedom makes greater freedom possible for the next choice. Suppose your parents have asked you to be home at a certain hour. You are "free" to reject or conform to this demand. If you *choose* to comply, thus building up confidence in yourself, you undoubtedly will enlarge your area of freedom. Thus, as you exercise *some* freedom, you achieve *more* freedom because you accept increasing responsibility.

Nor is freedom "doing what you want to do." In fact, if you always had to do only what you wanted to do, the number of choices constantly confronting you would overwhelm you. One cannot live by whim and indecision. Moreover, the lack of human relationships implicit in this lack of responsibility for anyone but yourself would leave you feeling very much alone. There is no freedom in a vacuum.

Freedom is certainly not the opposite of responsibility. Freedom implies willingness to assume increasing responsibilities for your own life, for the welfare of others, and for the world. Your family is a launching platform. It sends you forth to discover ever-widening limits in your world.

You demonstrate *your* freedom in your growing capacity to take a hand in your own development.

Finally, freedom implies accepting the realities of life, not from blind necessity, but from choice. Throughout life, there will be restrictions on your freedom: your age, sex, health, economic status, skill, knowledge, interests, responsibilities assumed toward others. Within these limitations, however, there is always a margin where you are aware of alternatives among which you choose as you decide upon one course of action or another.

This acceptance of your limitations need not be a discouraged "giving up" because you have less than the other fellow! Limitations may, in fact, force you to accomplish more than if you had no limitations against which to struggle. Accept your limitations as your building blocks! If you were planning a house, you would decide on the material; then you would work within the limits of the wood, bricks, or cement blocks. You cannot fight reality if you want to become free and remain free. You must move forward or you will move backward.

What Is Discipline?

This concept of freedom calls for a redefinition of the word discipline. Discipline means to learn, not to punish. Everyone wants discipline because he wants to know what is expected of him. He obtains a feeling of security by knowing what his limits are and knowing when he is successfully living within them. It is ego-bolstering to everyone to accomplish what is expected of him: one is stimulated to continue acceptable behavior.

Through effective discipline, an individual gradually learns

98

what he must and must not do to be an acceptable member of his family, school, campus, job, and neighborhood. Clearly, discipline is something a teenager must do to himself; it is not something done to him. For example, if he does not discipline his behavior, he may have an accident because he drove too fast or may fail the course because he did not study.

Naturally, not every family, school, employer, or community has this conception of discipline. In some situations, to discipline means to punish. In other situations, discipline problems arise because confusion exists between what is accepted as "right" and what is disapproved as "wrong." Especially when a person is new in a school, job, or community, he may become a discipline problem because he did the "wrong" thing before he had an opportunity to learn the "right" behavior.

Parental expectations vary. Sooner or later, teenagers ponder the fact that methods of discipline and standards of behavior expected of them vary from family to family. These differences exist because people are different—they expect different things of one another. In one family, parents make regulations and expect obedience. In another family, parents make no regulations and are not certain what they expect. In some families, parents seem to expect now one type of behavior, now another. On the whole, if parents are explicit and consistent in a few fair and simple standards, teenagers feel secure. If discipline is firm, but friendly, if parents, even when they say "no," can be loving and understanding, a teenager not only knows what is expected of him, but he feels that his parents are capable and willing and loving enough to guide him.

Teenagers cannot grow up without, every day of their lives, responding to discipline, both imposed from without and self-imposed. Inevitably, this fact rouses some hostility toward adults and toward the world. Struggling to meet "requirements" occasionally makes life difficult at best. Even with kindly, patient parents, virtually all teenagers feel, now and then, that the world is unfair and their parents unjust. Probably every teenager sometimes thinks, or even says, "Wait till I grow up, I'll show you"—or "I'll get even some day."

If these feelings can be accepted and talked out in families with good grace and humor, then—given time and affection —ordinary resentments disappear. In fact, teenagers can even learn to laugh at some of their resentments!

Teenagers can yield to demands most surely if they have been treated in their family as persons who are loved and valued. Then they *want* to respond to demands and to be the kind of person their parents and family will love. They *want* to use their abilities because they have been encouraged to use them and have been led to believe that use of them will win a cordial response from others.

Teenagers learn to control themselves, to assume responsibilities, and to yield to the rights of others largely through the experience of having their own rights respected, through knowing that they are being trusted with responsibilities, and that they are loved just as they are. Only when someone knows that he is worthwhile because he is loved and lovable is he capable of responding to others or of learning —either from people or from books.

Most parents make *some* rules in order to help a teenager understand what is expected of him. Aside from these, many
100

parents say, the best way for teenagers to learn about behavior is to experience a wide variety of behavior patterns
in the home—to become interested in behavior rather than
fearful of it. A teenager whose parents feel this way has
probably lived through family arguments, expressions of im-
patience and some upheaval—and learned that these clear
the air! His parents say that it is better to "blow off steam"
in what looks like exasperation than to hold back fears and
resentments which only crop out later in disguise!

Parents who have this kind of relationship with teenagers
will probably treat teenagers as they would their adult
friends. They may say, for example, "I'm sorry I acted that
way! I should have been more thoughtful." These parents
believe that if parents can admit their mistakes and talk
about their problems young people will not be afraid of
making their own mistakes. They learn that affection, love,
even devotion sometimes involve need for forgiveness! All
of us make mistakes. We resolve to do better next time;
there is no guilty brooding when one can confidently seek—
and find—forgiveness.

Parents who are completely themselves around young
people give young people the courage to be *themselves*.
Teenagers can *move out*, from such a family experience,
toward others. They have learned to accept people as they
are—just as they expect people to accept *them* as they are.

Can *you* allow your parents to be themselves—human
beings with problems, needs—and temperaments—different
from yours perhaps? In some homes, parents are automa-
tons: mothers are thought of as handy instruments to have
around for feeding, cleaning, and general errand-running;
fathers are useful as a source of money for clothing, amuse-

101

ments, and the family car—or as a last resort if mothers have refused permission for something. How does this make them feel?

In other homes, parents are expected to be reasonable facsimiles of perfection: always loving, kind, and gentle, even when they are dead tired, have just had a tooth pulled or have a headache. Some teenagers doubt their parents' love if parents do not live up to these unrealistic expectations. Can you grant your parents the right to be human—even to make mistakes—as you do?

Moments of tension between parents and teenagers are inevitable. If hostility can "blow itself out," teenagers are less likely to need "to get back at" people because they see themselves as victims of unjust punishment. However, if teenagers develop permanent fear-guilt–hostility feelings—these are not the result of momentary tensions; they are of long standing. They may reflect parental expectations arising in infancy—often, without a parent's conscious knowledge. Almost always, parents want to do "what is best" for the child. Yet one parent may have expected bodily control of a child when he was too young to exercise it. Another may have punished a child for temper tantrums when he was too immature to learn emotional control. Thus, gradually, parents build up feelings of rage and failure in a child.

Methods of control which make use of threats or call normal outbursts of rage "wicked" also, unwittingly, "knock the props" from under a child. For example, in response to a father's attitude—"He's got to learn," what a child learns is "I have to do this because Dad's around." But Dad isn't going to be present forever—and then what guide has

102

a growing boy or girl? Your major aim is not to "behave"
out of fear, but rather to be able to say "no" and "don't" to
yourself when no adults are around to stop undesirable behavior—and to say "do" to yourself when no one is around
to make you do as you should.

Two of the most precious qualities parents can teach
young people are confidence and courage. These are built
on unconditioned love. Should a child be told, as he dis-
obeys, "If you do that, Daddy won't love you," what the
child learns is that *he* is "bad" and unlovable—not that *what
he does* is bad. A child must feel sure of his parents' love—
no strings attached! He must be corrected for his acts, but
learn that he himself is treasured: "I don't like your behavior
and I don't want it repeated," not "I don't like you; you
are bad." Around a child's fears of losing parental love can
develop fears and hostilities that last a lifetime. On the
other hand, when a child can count on affection, warmth,
and a feeling of belonging, he can face his mistakes and not
be afraid.

If adults you know are unable so to work with you, remember that adults can teach you courage and confidence
only if they have it themselves. The more they have, the
better will they be able to build it in you. The less they
have, the more mistakes they will make in all their human
relationships. Whatever mistakes parents and other adults
have made in the past with you, the present and future are
still available to you. The past need not "get you down"!

Most parents would probably agree that no teenager is
innately perverse and that no one can be coerced or punished into "being good." Yet there is a type of parent who
demands absolute authority and unquestioning submission.

Teenagers say that some adults seem to distrust human nature so much that they cannot believe that a young person will do anything decent or right unless browbeaten into it. They say that this attitude is the explanation for the stern and rigid rules emphasized by such parents.

Children of such parents begin to regard them only as authorities to fear, deceive, placate, hate, or envy—not as helpful personalities who praise and reward effort, who encourage and comfort in time of fear or failure. Actually, this kind of parent is teaching children that he or she will "love" them only if the children "keep their place." The "good" child—to such a parent—is "the doormat," the obedient, self-deprecating person who is humbly grateful to parents for their sacrifices, apparently ready to believe that parents— later teachers and employers—always "know best." In reality, such an individual is full of irrational hostility!

If parental controls are too severe, if a child is *continually* thwarted and *repeatedly* punished, if he feels unloved and powerless, his resentment leads to sulkiness, repression, the storing up of grudges and desire for revenge. Years of injustice and wounds to a person's dignity affect him more than a single terrible experience. Such a person may tend to spend the rest of his life plotting how to "get even."

Another parent may be so puzzled by this business of bringing up children that he refuses to tell a child what to do or he forces choices on him too early—like the parent who never changed her two-year-old's diaper without asking him whether he wanted it changed! Teenagers *want* guidance and direction in setting limits to their behavior. In fact, they learn to know what to expect of themselves partly as they understand, gradually, what their parents expect of

104

them. Granted, it is not easy for parents to learn when and how to give or withhold direction or limitation!

However, some parents exercise no control and set no limits. They may explain themselves by saying that they are afraid they will lose the young person's love if they punish or restrict him. Actually, parents who are unable to discipline their children are usually unable to discipline themselves. Moreover, a parent who truly "loves" the young person and wants him to be happy, cares about what a young person does. He does not abdicate his responsibility to guide and "stand by."

Still another parent confuses a teenager: he expects—or tolerates—first one kind of behavior, then exactly the opposite kind in the same situation, depending on the mood of the moment. One day he may punish a teenager severely for some behavior, the next day, completely disregard the identical behavior. Or, he may "change his mind" if a teenager teases, becomes stubborn, or refuses to do what he is told. This parent usually cannot bear to say "no" and stick to it even when he knows he is right! Therefore, he has to work himself into a lather before a teenager understands when he really means something. Is it surprising that this teenager seldom takes rules seriously? He has learned in his family that there are few rules which cannot be broken if he refuses to obey them!

Or, perhaps two parents disagree on a teenager's behavior. Then a teenager either does not know what to expect, or he plays off one parent against another. A child of such parents is insecure; he does not know what kind of person he is supposed to be.

Other parents are so overprotective that a teenager has

no life of his own. Parents grant him no privacy, demand that he share all his plans and hopes, that he give a "blow-by-blow" account of "all you did today"—then, generally, they criticize or offer unwanted advice. Is it any wonder that teenagers try to protect themselves by not telling "the truth"?

Some kinds of parents demand too much of a teenager—too much love, too much success, too perfect behavior. For example, they may expect him *always* to perform as he *sometimes* performs; they may become hurt and angry at all backsliding. Do these parents realize that even adults under the influence of fatigue or emotional tension regress to somewhat infantile behavior? No adult always lives on the level of his professed principles. Yet each of us would like to be judged by his occasional success in rising above himself rather than by that more common weakness, falling below the standards one has set oneself!

Finally, some parents develop in teenagers a feeling of unworthiness, as well as injustice, because they fail to behave to him with the same level of courtesy and consideration they expect from him. There is the parent who never expresses appreciation to a teenager for help given—or the parent who suddenly interrupts a four-year-old absorbed in play, demanding, "I want you!" then slaps the child for replying, "I want myself!"

Difficulties such as these are not confined to one economic level; they certainly are not found only in homes where cash "is short." In fact, the root of many teenagers' serious difficulties frequently lies in too much money or overemphasis on material values, whether this condition results from wealth or from both parents working because they "need" more material things. The "poor little rich—or overindulged—child" may be the truly neglected, unloved child. Where homes are run on the principle that a great deal of spending money, many things, hired companionship, and supervision will result in happy children, one actually finds many insecure, unhappy young people.

Obviously, a teenager who has had these experiences will be confused and miserable about his relationship to authority. Many school, college, and job failures stem, partly, from inability to establish consistent and good-willed feelings toward people in authority. Over a period of time, with love and sensitive understanding, such people may be helped to accept necessary authority. They may also learn that everyone sometimes resents authority; but that his desire for independence is accompanied by a desire for dependence. There are two sides to everyone's nature: the desire to do what he wants and to do what will please others.

A teenager also needs facts about the exercise of authority: namely, that adults sometimes see behavior consequences which teenagers have not had enough experience to anticipate. Therefore, adults must sometimes, for teenagers' own physical safety—or to convert them into tolerable members of a group!—restrict their impulses or unbridled desires and *require* that they develop habits which "make no sense" to them.

Other school, college, or work failures result from a teenager's inability to use his capacities. This inability may be due to emotional conflict in his family, perhaps to an open and obvious struggle, sometimes to a hidden, partly unconscious one. Suppose that a person had a father or mother who completely dominated him or who was oversolicitous or who played favorites and liked a brother or sister better than him. He resented these attitudes. But he repressed his resentment because, as explained in a previous chapter, he disapproved of feelings he considered unacceptable or he feared his negative feelings. The emotion doesn't go away because a person refuses to recognize it! It makes trouble: by his failure to do his work in school, an individual "gets back" at his parents. Resentment against his family comes out in his losing interest in school, college, or work, in his inability to concentrate or to follow directions; in his going to pieces on an examination or in process of learning a new skill, or in his indulging in such unacceptable behavior or language in and around school, college, or his job that he brings down on his head the wrath of the authorities and the disapproval of his classmates or coworkers.

With a few teenagers, rebellion against what they consider the injustice of their parents is so all-embracing that they are unhappy in a school or college course or a career solely because their parents approve it. They feel compelled to oppose all evidences of authority—even parental guidance —because their need to "get back" at their parents is so great that anything less than an open rebellion is interpreted as meek submission! Such young people need to learn that it is possible for mature people to make choices, acquire independence, and still be on good terms with their families!

To want to do what is acceptable is normal. Every teenager understands that some rules are necessary—not only to teach him what is expected of him in the future, but to teach him, today, to get along without pain or friction in his family and with his peers. Most teenagers want to be "good" in the sense of wanting to take on the ways of people around them whom they admire; they want to follow the rules and customs of their homes, schools, employers, and communities. To do the acceptable thing is the normal person's aim.

Teenagers must have contact with adults who *earn* their respect and love if they are to be able to take on the ways of adults. Teenagers can identify with adults only if they "feel good" about being like them. They must *want* to adopt given standards.

The standards teenagers are most likely to "take on" are not those "preached" to them, but those which they understand because they have had a part in developing them. Teenagers learn what is expected of a good, "free" person in our society by being kept "on their toes," experimenting in doing interesting things together, taking responsibility, sacrificing personal desires to a common enterprise, relying on themselves to carry through a job, meeting success and failure realistically, and earning praise justifiably.

This is the essence of discipline: to develop, together with adults, standards which they can work and live by because they have tested them and found that they make sense. Thus, agreement is reached on realistic standards—geared to teenagers, not to angels! Adults need not fear that this will mean lack of standards. On the contrary, teenagers need to realize that they are often harder on themselves than adults would dare be; for those who deviate from standards set, teenagers more than "make the punishment fit the crime"!

Finally, teenagers need to realize that not everyone is able to meet acceptable standards of behavior. We must all learn to understand the difference between behavior which is healthy—no matter how difficult it may be to live with— and behavior which is due to an excessively disturbed, un-

happy past. A disturbed person needs the professional help
of psychiatrists and mental health clinics. However, if his
classmates are mature enough to understand, he desperately
needs their respect, sympathy, and affection.

His associates may have to inhibit his behavior and stop
some of his actions; but if their feelings about *him* are
"right"—if they do not harbor anger, fury, or excessive an-
noyance against him—he will listen to their hearts as well
as their tongues. Such mature young people can truly
"stand by" someone in trouble and can help classmates,
teachers, club leaders, or other important people in his life
to understand his problems. As incidents pile up in which
the disturbed person finds himself approved, commended,
successful, accepted, liked, wanted, able to accomplish assigned or chosen tasks and responsibilities, these experiences
begin to undo past harm. Gradually, with professional help
and the sensitive understanding of his associates, he may
be able to achieve everyone's normal state of health—cooperative social behavior.

Your Brothers' and Sisters' Point of View

Nothing so predisposes people to understand as making
them feel that they are understood. If you try to understand your brothers' and sisters' point of view as you have
just tried to understand your parents', you may find much
in common with them. You will certainly find them more
disposed to understand you.

You have loves and hates in common. You will probably discover that each of you harbors some fears and resentments against one another. These may be rooted in
an injustice experienced in the past for which there was a

110

reason, but which no one now can change. Perhaps, when the second child came along, your parents concentrated so devotedly upon the infant that the oldest felt crowded out and rejected—and still "hates" the second child—or, at least, isn't always sure he really likes him! Or, suppose parents turned the middle child into a servant of the baby— or expected the rest of the family to be like the oldest who does everything well! As a result, everyone feels some resentment, some desire for revenge—together with the powerlessness of one who thinks he has suffered injustice but cannot alter conditions.

Along with the resentment, you all love the same people— one another and your parents. You're capable of loving and hating at the same time! In fact, you wouldn't be normal if you didn't! This is also true of your parents. They love you—but, let's face it, there's a little hatred there too. Sometimes they would like to bat your head against the nearest wall! When they let you know this, what do you do? You hate right back. You'd strangle them cheerfully if you could get away with it!

However, when you know that you are hated, you are also insecure. Perhaps you become silent and morose—or you rebel and plan to avenge yourself on that "big bully," your father! More likely, you blame your brothers and sisters— they are the favorites or they got you into trouble!

What do you like about your brothers and sisters? Most important, of course, is that, in spite of the mixed feelings which everyone has sometimes, basically they like you. You teach one another how to get along with people. Everyone learns how to give and take, how to compromise and cooperate, how to be a good loser, how to stand up for his rights firmly, but without anger. He finds out that everyone is different, yet that each is interesting.

Some are loud and quick-tempered and always "into something"; others are quiet, easygoing, and put off doing things. Some like to do things with their hands; others like to read; others go in for sports. It's sometimes difficult to live with different tastes, abilities, and dispositions—but when you all enjoy one another instead of feeling that you must compete with one another, compare yourself with someone else, or all be alike—then you learn what is meant by "it takes all kinds to make a world" and you begin to appreciate people because their very differences interest you.

Many families sit down together regularly, generally once a week, and talk out their feelings. If you present a problem honestly and thoughtfully, but not angrily, you're not being unfair to your brothers and sisters in presenting *anything* which keeps you from getting along better. There are many different reasons for misunderstandings and quarrels. Try to figure out the causes; maybe your family can help you in getting rid of them.

At least, it helps to get complaints off your chest without causing hard feelings! Your parents may even change their way of doing some things! Perhaps, unknowingly, they were overprotecting you ever since you had pneumonia last year—but it makes your sister think you "get by with everything!" Perhaps Dad did have a sneaking feeling that, because you didn't like football, you might develop into a sissy! Or maybe Mother boasted too much about your high grades —and your brother resents "the model guy."

You share so much. Brother-sister troubles can last a lifetime. But they don't have to if you understand the reasons for them and do something to smooth the rough spots. You need to know, when you are angry with your brothers and sisters, that you love them at the same time. Living together, helping one another, sharing disappointments, fun, even the same parents—these things make love stronger than occasional hates. Love definitely *is* stronger than hate!

It takes some teenagers a long time to learn that their parents have enough love for *all* their children—and for each other. It is difficult for other teenagers to understand that parents may love one child in one way and another in a different way, enjoy one child for certain reasons and another for different reasons. Those teenagers who never learn may go through life feeling, deep down, that a brother or sister was favored—consequently, was valued more than they. This feeling builds resentment, thus threatens self-respect.

No matter where you come in the family, things look tough sometimes. Your position in the family is determined for you; there is nothing you can do about that. But you can see the advantages in your position instead of thinking only of its drawbacks! These are some ways suggested by teenagers: "Having an older sister helps me; she explains to Mother why I do some of the things I do." A fellow said that it was fun helping "the younger kids make friends"; he added that his sister looked up to him because "I can wise her up to what to do or not to do." "Everyone wants to be in the crowd, so when I told my younger brothers not to wear dungarees to High School—the girls wouldn't like it— they listened; though they'd argued with Mom when she tried to tell them." A middle brother said, "You can be an example for the younger one, not obviously, but you do it

113

unconsciously; you want to do something, then you think you'd better not—it makes you feel good when a younger brother wants to be like you!" Most important is the fact that, in a family, you have people who love you, are interested in you, want to share your joys and sorrows. A family can give you that comfortable feeling of "belonging" somewhere, of really counting with people!

The Mother As a Woman

A recent study of personality development in 300 girls,* aged ten-and-a-half to twenty years, from many types of backgrounds, showed that girls are, above all, confused "about the feminine role." Considering the number of books and articles currently appearing on the confusion of grown women about their place in life, this is not surprising. Young people of both sexes need to face frankly: what do you expect of a girl, a wife, and a mother? Is she to be a glamor girl, a tomboy in blue jeans and boys' shirts, an intellectual companion, a homemaker, a personal maid, a child guidance expert?

Being a wife and mother in the world today is an important responsibility. She is visualized as a nutrition expert, cook, dietitian, laundress, economist, valet, personal maid, purchasing agent, social secretary, trained nurse, hostess, child psychologist, interior decorator, fashion designer, personnel relations expert, diplomat, watchdog of government, and student of international affairs. In addition, most mothers need to be chauffeurs and mechanics. Soon, in

* Lawrence Frank et al., *Personality Development of Adolescent Girls,* Society for Research in Child Development, School of Medicine, Louisiana State University, New Orleans, 1951, Vol. XVI, No. 53.

114

fact, they may need to pilot their families in planes! Moreover, since parents are supposed "to share their children's
interests," mothers also need to learn to play boys' games
because, in our world, fathers are generally away during
most of the children's waking hours.

Finally, all their lives, some mothers will work on jobs as
well as in their homes. Some women will work because
they must; some because they like what they do. Some
women will mark time on a job until they marry; others will
build a career. Whether a woman marries, has a career or
both, it is not what she *does* that makes her feminine in the
true sense of the word; it is, rather, how she *feels* about
herself and her place as a woman.

A girl's and a boy's model for the feminine role, obviously,
is the mother in the family. If a mother feels overworked,
harried, guilty about tasks undone, she can hardly expect her
daughter to be enthusiastic about being a woman or her
son to rate women highly. This is the way a fourth grader
saw his mother: "A mother should be very kind and help us
with our homework when it is hard. She should make
breakfast, lunch and supper. She should take care of the
baby. She should try to understand everything we do and
another thing very important, she should try to help us to
grow up. If we have a pet, she should help us take care of
it. She should wash dishes, clothes, iron and cook. A
mother should let you stay up late. She should not work
too much. I'll never be a mother, will you?"

If this is what children understand by being a woman,
no wonder a girl is reluctant to grow up and face life as a
woman—and no wonder a boy is glad he was born to be a
man! Some women do take being a woman, especially being

a mother, so seriously that they try too hard; they have become grim in their outlook on life. Lily Daché in her *Glamour Book* calls them the martyr mothers; they see themselves as slaves to their families. They could be different. Labor-saving devices make women's work less arduous than it was even a decade ago. Many women have free time in which to take part in voluntary activities in the community or to develop interests "on their own."

How a woman uses her time depends on what she considers important. The values she finds time for reveal her conception of herself. No one can tell a *particular* woman the components of her feminine role. Each must decide for herself what she puts first. She must set her own standards for family living—when she *has* a family—then constructively and flexibly organize her life so that, in addition, she has time and quiet leisure to grow in understanding of herself and others. The important thing is that she likes herself as she is—that she enjoys being a woman!

The way in which a woman regards herself inevitably affects the way a man regards himself as a man. If a woman relates to her husband with positiveness and warmth, if she considers her basic role that of bringing strength, security, and serenity to those about her, then her children and husband, in a warm, happy home, will probably develop warm, human qualities and a feeling for cooperation. They will consider these qualities important in themselves; they will see themselves as friendly, likable, cooperative, capable people. To have this example to follow is the surest method yet devised to ensure a girl's functioning at her best in her own home as well as in any business or profession she may enter or in any community she may live.

116

It is the most certain way of preparing a boy to seek these qualities in women and to treat as "successful" the woman who is loved and loving, accepted and accepting.

The Father As a Man

What mothers can give to children depends a great deal on the love and understanding husbands give to wives. Bringing up baby doesn't depend only on whether Father has a good job and can furnish a decent place to live with space for baby to play. Bringing up a child happily depends on parents' getting along happily together, with mutual respect for one another and for one another's skills and contributions in their common enterprise as well as mutual respect for the rights and privileges of every member of the family— mother, father, and child.

When father, mother, and child accept each other as full and equal members of the family circle, such home atmosphere creates a feeling of adequacy in the child—a sense of worth because he or she seems prized by *both* parents. The way in which a child handles his experiences—the way his personality shapes up—is dependent largely on the support, love, and guidance he or she receives from *both* parents in day-by-day events which are steppingstones to maturity.

Because a child desires to be like both Mother and Dad, his or her successes, failures, and important experiences are immeasurably enhanced by Father's interest, presence, and participation if these are naturally and freely offered. The father's role in setting a pattern of emotional warmth and friendly give-and-take with a girl is just as important as the manly habits which the boy who wants to be "like Daddy" must acquire from him. The adjustment of both children

117

in marriage may depend largely on the type of experience they had with their fathers.

Babies are not predisposed at birth to love their mothers more than their fathers. In fact, recent studies have shown that many attitudes toward oneself and other people come from childhood experiences with a *father*. Mother stands for home—protection and comfort. But Father represents the great outside world and, unconsciously, a person comes to expect from the outside world the treatment originally received from his father.

Therefore, in later life, an individual's reactions to teachers, friends, employers, business associates, religious and political affiliations tend to reflect the childish pattern of relationship with one's father. This fact may explain some hostilities and disillusionments. An easygoing father, especially if coupled with a mother who is the "executive type," can cause grown children to expect the wrong things from men and women—in marriage, job, or social relationships. For example, a young man may seek more strength in a wife than he finds. He feels let down because she's not like Mother. The real trouble is: he's too much like Father!

One young woman may expect to dominate men. Another may feel it necessary to build up her ego by belittling men to "get back" at a father who considered her unimportant. Still another may constantly compete with men—"the anything you can do, I can do better" attitude! Maybe she *is* better; but you don't make friends and influence people by proving to them that you are better than they. You don't even prove it to yourself! Trying to be like a man or better than a man can never be a satisfying experience for a woman.

Being a woman can be wonderful and exciting. If this is

what Father thinks, both a young man and a young woman need to know that. What Father thinks is particularly important to the future wife and mother. From Father she develops a pattern of what a husband and father will be like. If Father feels that being a woman is important, she will accept this as being the attitude of men in general and feel good about being a woman. A young man, in turn, will learn to estimate women as he sees his father estimate them.

The boy in the family learns what a man is by identifying with his father. Increasingly, fathers who have learned that even infants understand and interpret feelings attempt to develop genuine give-and-take relationships with their young sons and encourage boys to share their tasks and their enthusiasms. Thus, boys gradually learn to be like Daddy, from the day they go with him to the barber and want their curls cut off to be like him, through the years when they copy his clothes, want a workbench in the woodshop like his, learn from him to swim and pitch a ball, go fishing with him, seek his help in their algebra—and his experience with women!

What a father feels about a boy and how he acts toward him are of supreme importance in a boy's development—as in a girl's. Does the boy know with certainty that his father accepts him and loves him as he is—or does he feel that he is a disappointment to his father? Perhaps he's not going to "make the grade" for Harvard—and his father enrolled him the day that he first bent over his crib! Or does his father scold him for the hours he spends collecting bugs and watching birds when he should be out for football practice? Or does he resent his wanting to go to college because "I was out earning a living when I was your age"?

Does a father see himself as an important member of his family, an unimportant one, or the all-important one? Is he primarily the source of authority, of leniency, of money, of courage, of comfort? Does he assume a share in all family responsibilities or is he to be shielded from arduous tasks, spared tales of his children's deeds and misdeeds, in fact, tenderly waited upon and ministered to? Or is he to be loftily disregarded as weighty decisions are made save when these involve cash which he must supply? What does a boy learn from his father about what a man is and how a man behaves?

"Belonging" to a Family

If you have a real "home," where parents are sincerely interested in you, where you all "belong" to one another, a happy home with lots of laughter in it, then you can build a "self" and grow up, secure, regardless of today's headlines. Sometimes young people and their parents worry too much about the insecurity of the modern world. Beyond the garden hedge—or at the outer door of the apartment—there has always been insecurity. If it wasn't the H bomb, it was plague and famine! If it wasn't the Russians, it was the Seminoles or the Navajos! If it wasn't death and taxes, it was witches and seven-year locusts!

Sometimes material things seem too important to family living. True, you live in a country where, for the first time in history, man is emerging from chronic poverty to a level where he is reasonably certain that he will not be hungry or cold—a country which offers him, for a price within his income, all sorts of wonderful things he can share with his family. However, nothing is more important to "self"-

development than a satisfying home life! Home is a testing-ground. Here you discover how to get along smoothly with other people and can practice what you learn. Whether you are an only child or one of a dozen, the way you get along with your family affects the way you adjust to other people—your friends, classmates, coworkers, employer, your wife, or husband, and your own children.

Peaceful and happy coexistence means something different in every family because of the necessity of respecting the individuality of all members of the family. Yet, there are general principles which you would probably want to follow if you could choose the family in which to grow up. Whether the family is rich or poor, whether it has been broken by death or divorce, is relatively unimportant compared to: is there love and friendliness, respect for each individual, confidence in one another, integrity in all relationships, a sense of security and of purpose?

Friendliness! How simple—how necessary—and how often neglected! Respect for one another—no one person's pattern of living dominant, neither father's, mother's nor child's! Confidence in one another—belief in each other and freedom for development given to whatever degree each can "take it"! Compromise when necessary, but not the type of compromise which "waters down" everyone's ideas and interests so that no spontaneity is left! No personal attacks on one another—not everybody jumping in and fanning one person's irritation into a major disturbance! Only one person gets angry at a time! Individuality is respected; there is intimacy but no prying. Each person has privacy because all know that it can be genuine torment never to be able to get out of sight of other human beings. Each knows that he is close to his family, though separate. They are "with him" when he needs them; but he is not abjectly dependent on them. In such a family, you learn usefulness and cooperation, brotherhood, maturity. With such experience, you are safe; for you will probably do as adults do, not as they say—just as young people have always done!

People Are Important

No ONE can develop a "self" in a vacuum; everyone needs other people. Together with and because of other people, you laugh and cry, love and work, enjoy and suffer to the limit of your capacity. To say that an individual and society are interrelated is not theory; you *know* that what people think, say, and feel about you is vital.

123

You are conscious of your "self" as you see yourself reflected in the way others see you—as beautiful or ugly, popular or unpopular, bright or dumb, loved or tolerated or not loved, shy or sparkling. You resent your limitations because they jeopardize others' good opinion of you; you develop skills and accomplishments to make yourself an enjoyable companion to people whose good opinion you crave. All you learn pays off in developing a personality which wins a friendly response from others.

You Need Friends

Everyone wants to feel accepted in some friendship group. It is important to be "in" a group at school and college, at work, or in your community—preferably, most people think, in a group which "rates" high in the opinion of people whose estimates you value. You are willing and eager to develop ways of behaving which will ensure that "the crowd" really wants you.

Particularly if you are new in a community, how do you gain acceptance—or "make" the crowd? Dan, a popular junior in high school, says, "I think any crowd will take you in if you're friendly and fun to be with. But don't try to force your way in or oversell yourself—or try to break up the crowd by rushing one or two in it! Some people think they'll get 'in' if they can be intimate with one or another already in a crowd. That's wrong. If a new person attaches himself to one person only, the rest of the gang thinks he's trying to take that person away. The gang becomes suspicious of the new person. The one he is attached to can't help him because if he pushed too hard for the new person, the gang might think he liked the new person better than he
124

did them. Then they'd throw him out! He's afraid of this
—so, generally, he won't take chances. When he finds out
that the gang feels suspicious of the newcomer's actions, he
probably breaks off with the new person. He doesn't want
to lose his old friends for someone new whom he may like,
but isn't sure about!

"It's much better, when you're in a new place, not to try
to crash the first crowd you meet. Take your time! Look
everybody over—and when you see a crowd you think you'd
like, be friendly with all of them. Help them with their
homework or some school affair—maybe decorate or take
tickets or clean up—or help putter with their cars. Show
that you like the things that they do—and are good at doing
them. Don't push yourself obviously, but work at it! Offer
to do things for them that they'd appreciate. It's up to you
to make half-way gestures!"

Peg, Dan's girl friend, broke in to add, "Look at me. I
came here in September—it's my junior year in high school.
I found out that the crowd I liked were interested in basketball. My Dad likes basketball—and I love it. I began going to games—and talking to the crowd I liked—just cas-
ually. During one game, they were talking about next
week's game—away from home. They wanted to go—but
there was no public transportation to the town where the
game was. I offered to ask my Dad if he'd take all of them
in the station wagon. He did—and when we won the game,
Dad was so excited that he suggested they all come home for
hamburgers. After that, they've always included me in the
crowd!"

"Maybe the crowd you like is interested in bowling, football, skating, the church choir, the local Youth Center, danc-

ing, or clothes. You have to be *really* interested in and able to join in on what they like—at least have some worthwhile ideas—so they'll respect you for what you can do. You can't pretend! If they find you've 'got something,' they'll take you in!"

"Of course, you're not going to like everyone in the crowd the same amount," Peg warns. "You have to be careful about that—at first, anyway—because they'll stick together against you. They've been together a long time and that means there is something between them you can't share. The gang I go with has been together since they were seventh-grade kids. I like some of them better than others. Of the girls, I like Pat best because she's so sensible—or maybe it's because she and I are the only ones who aren't in the local Sub-Debs. That's an exclusive club for which you must 'receive a bid.' Pat says that, though she was with the gang through Junior High, her parents made her turn down the bid which came the summer afterward because they considered Sub-Debs snobbish. At first, Pat says, she was mad at her parents—'but now I've learned to like people for what they are, not for what they're in—or what they have, like money.' Anyway, Pat's my favorite—but I get along with all of them."

Friendship groups provide opportunity to try out your feelings, interests, and abilities. You learn how you really appear to other people—and you try to make this reality as acceptable as possible!

Sometimes there are group decisions about manners, clothes, speech, sophistication, glamor, sex appeal, "being a good sport." These standards are so clearly understood that, frequently, they are "taken for granted" by group members.

126

They need not be stated in words. What a group "takes a stand on" may puzzle adults, but to the group, its decisions are obvious: through group decisions, teenagers bolster one another in a frightening adult world, in resisting too many adult demands. What a group considers important enough to "take a stand on" varies according to group members' ages, family, economic or community backgrounds, happy or unhappy experiences with adults at home, school, college, or work.

The closer knit a group, the more it influences its members to conform when it "takes a stand." When *your* friendship group makes a decision, it expects you to behave as it would like you to behave. Perhaps you abide by the group's decision and do what is expected because you agree with the decision and *wish* to abide by it. You may abide by it in spite of the fact that you disagree with it because you are afraid of social ostracism if you do not comply. You may flaunt the group's decision because you consider it "idiotic" and you "want everyone to know it." Or, when you disagree, you may discuss the situation calmly and openly, letting the group know—in friendly fashion—why you disagree and feel that you must act differently. Then, with no apologies, recriminations, or bravado, you go your way. Each teenager must decide, at some point, if a group is to be his supreme authority or if he will stand for what he believes—against group pressure if necessary.

It takes courage to maintain an opinion or to follow a course of action contrary to that of a group important to you. Pressure to conform is strong and risk of rejection by the group seems so great that you sometimes compromise. For example, you do as the group wishes; then, when you are alone, you find that "you" really wanted to oppose the group. You feel that the group was unfair; *you* aren't like that; your real "self" knew better. Do you then excuse yourself or try to think up "good" reasons to explain your inability to think and act for yourself?

Suppose some insecure gossip in the group has been poisoning the rest of the gang about the "faults" of some friend of yours. Do you gleefully join "in righteous wrath" to victimize another human being? If so, why? Perhaps it is important to your prestige in school, college, or community that you be considered "in" this particular group. If they say you're "just a dope if you don't fall in with this deal," you "go along" because you are afraid of being considered an outsider.

In this case, the group has become your final "authority" because you feel "safe" and "acceptable" only when the group approves of you. You may even be afraid that, although you are inside, you are not very important to them, that "they" may not like you and keep you inside. You may feel lonely and afraid they'll turn on you if you don't join them in turning on someone else. You're not the only one! Many people share your fears. Read the play *The Ins and Outs.* *

Sometimes teenagers yield to group pressure because people actually mean little to them. Such teenagers may have been taught, early in life, to be "nice," to share possessions, or to be quiet when others talk. This does not necessarily mean that they have learned to be genuinely concerned about others, or that they take pleasure in companionship,

* Nora Stirling, *The Ins and Outs,* National Association for Mental Hygiene, New York, 1949.

128

or that they listen thoughtfully to what people say, or that they know how to give and take, or that they can so prune their personal ambitions that they do not hurt others.

If you *really care* when a person is being wronged, if you have developed sympathy and ability to put yourself in another's place, you do not "turn away" from a friend. Your group is not some impersonal force which can *make* you do something you consider dishonest, unfair, or unkind to another human being. You know that group approval can be bought at too high a price.

If you know that you are a warm, friendly person whom other people enjoy, that you have interests and abilities to contribute to a group, then you see your friendship group as a collection of individuals whom you enjoy because of your mutual companionship, understanding, and shared interests. You are not one of those unhappy individuals who fears the opinion of others too much to be yourself. Once you are convinced of what is right for *you*, you may suffer, for a time, for your opinion—but you are true to yourself.

You Need Group Approval

Everyone's happiness is largely dependent on how well he or she gets along with people, individually and in groups. All your life you will be living in and working with groups of people. You had your first experiences in group living in your family. Perhaps you borrowed or adopted your parents' standards for group living. Sometimes they exhorted you to do so; sometimes you wanted to follow their example because you "felt good" about the way people treated one another in your family. As you entered school, different groups pressured you to conform to *their* standards.

Teachers wanted you to work hard and be obedient; the gang expected you, at least occasionally, *not* to obey every adult command, not to work all the time or to be too "good."

From each group, the penalty for not conforming was rejection and disapproval. The reward was acceptance and approval. If the latter was not forthcoming, you sometimes settled temporarily for lack of disapproval and "being let alone." All your life this dilemma will confront you: to conform or not to conform—or—to what degree to conform!

The less emotionally mature a teenager is, the more likely he is to drift into extremes of rebellion or conformity. Small children, for example, are intensely and grimly concerned about their rights; they resist attempts to force them to conform. As children grow, however, they become *great* conformists! Approval is very important to them; if they see parents or teachers turn from them in disapproval, they are seized by unreasoning fear—they might have to face life alone!

This fear persists in many adults. Such insecure persons *may* realize that they risk losing their individuality if they follow group leadership *blindly;* yet, they are so afraid of being cut off from the group! They fear loneliness more. For many people, this is a specter from which to flee at any cost. Artie Shaw, the band leader, wrote: "Although I wasn't consciously aware of it, what I needed most of all in the world was a friend—someone I could talk to, someone with whom I could share my ideas, not only about music but about all sorts of things which were beginning to interest me.... For there is nothing on land or sea, not death or taxes, not misfortune or calamity, not disaster or catastrophe, neither thirst, nor famine, nor even unrequited love

as sung by all the poets . . . that compares with this aim-
less, nerve-racking restlessness, this frightful, feverishly
brooding lassitude shot through with pale gleams of sickly
flickering energy, this pallid, shadowy visitor who makes his
home in the lukewarm vacuum of lethargy, this gaunt and
hollow-eyed monstrosity called Loneliness."

People fear also what a group can do to them if they do
not conform. After all, a group may withhold food, shelter,
and clothing if a person does not work for a living, may deny
him freedom if he breaks its laws or, more subtly, may withhold status and acceptance, may shame and humiliate him,
or may, by refusing to listen to or appreciate him, deny him
the right to express himself and his abilities.

This latter threat—to label someone a failure—is particularly potent in our society where success is so important.
Many a teenager feels that, if he doesn't "make" the "gang,"
the team, the fraternity, the promotion, the class office he
wants, his "self" is threatened! *He* feels disgraced, both
because he fears the low estimate which this judgment of
others places upon him and because their judgment lowers
his estimate of himself.

The unrealistic standards set by demands in our society
that we be satisfied with nothing less than constant and
brilliant success go far toward explaining most teenagers'
negative reaction to failure. Everyone is bound to fail sometimes. If only we could regard failure as an opportunity to
learn instead of fearing it, hating ourselves or blaming others
for it, or pretending that we never failed at all!!

Being a member of a family, a "crowd," a club, a school
or college class, a church, or other group *does* involve sacrifices and restrictions on your freedom of thought and action.

However, you obtain food, shelter, clothing, and protection from enemies and disease through *cooperative* activities— not by facing the world alone. Only through people can you satisfy your needs for status and identity, love and acceptance, achievement, and new experiences—needs as essential as life itself. Through personal contacts and friendly relationships with others, you learn to express your thoughts and feelings and to develop your potentialities. In fact, a human being becomes "human" through human association; no one develops a "self" in isolation.

You Need to Face Your Real Feelings

Human nature is not all sweetness and light. Nor is it all bitterness and darkness. Many factors go into the making of *your* unique personality. You need to see your "self" openly and honestly—and state what kind of person you are. When your "self" is thus expressed—pinned down, as it were, then respect it! Do not attack it, criticize it, or belittle it; this is "you" at the moment! To paraphrase—

> You ain't what you ought to be
> You ain't what you want to be
> You ain't what you're going to be—
> But, thank God, you ain't what you used to be!

To express your *real* self, you must first clarify your thoughts and feelings. You cannot express what you want to say unless you know what you actually are thinking and feeling. Can you be honest about your thoughts and feelings? Everyone has both positive and negative ones. Everyone prefers to acknowledge only the positive ones.

If one could only rid himself of the "undesirable" ones by denying or belittling them or diverting attention from them!

132

However, there are times when you want to say, in words or actions, "I am angry—I am afraid—right now, I hate you—I've been made to feel like a fool—I want the same thing my brother does and I'm jealous because he got it—I don't think I can do that."

Naturally, at different chronological ages, people express their feelings differently. Extermination is a small child's response to fear or frustration: he howls, "I hate you and I'll kill you." A youngster may "get back at" or exploit others; he may act out feelings like "I'll do to you what others did to me" or "I don't like you—but I'll use you." A teen-ager attempts to tolerate the new and frightening; however, sometimes "tolerance" of a new person is actually indiffer-ence—or is tinged with the patronizing "He's different—but we appreciate his worth." A more mature reaction is genu-ine eagerness to try something new and willingness to allow someone to develop in his unique fashion: "Be yourself. We like you."

Chronological maturity does not guarantee emotional maturity; so some people never grow beyond an infantile level of expression. Only when you know what you want to say and recognize what you are saying can you take responsi-bility for what you actually do say.

The mature person tries to face his "good" and "bad" feel-ings positively. He "controls" them by so channeling "bad" feelings that they do not hurt others or himself and by us-ing "good" feelings to furnish energy which drives him to fulfill his ambitions.

Your fears. The feelings most difficult to recognize and face are one's fears and prejudices. Everyone suffers from real or fancied fears. The most persistent fears *stem from* fear of not being loved, especially by one's parents; for ex-

133

ample, insecure teenagers may fear that, if they fail in school or college or on the job, parents or important adults will withdraw their love. This fear is often so deep as to paralyze effort.

Many teenagers fear inadequacy, bodily injury, fire, traffic, confinement, attack by others, or changes due to physical growth. Everyone, to an extent, fears "difference" as he faces the conflict arising between adults' and teenagers' standards. He is in a dilemma because he wants to become independent of his parents and accepted as one of the gang; yet he needs to depend on his parents for comfort, reassurance, and affection. He wants to act, talk, dress, and be like the gang; but, if his parents disapprove of the gang, he's afraid to be like the gang—yet afraid to be different.

How does a teenager recognize his fears? The following questions summarize many methods: Does he pretend they aren't there by chanting to himself "I'm not scared" when all the time his stomach is turning over? Does he have too many upset stomachs, headaches, nightmares, facial twitching, stuttering—or too much nail biting? Does he daydream excessively? Is he much shyer and more timid than other people his age? Is he "afraid to open his mouth," afraid to express an opinion, afraid to do or say or be anything except what he's been told? Does he have "a chip on his shoulder," boast, bully, fight, gossip more than most people his age?

Such a person can learn to face and resolve his fears thus: Know what you are really afraid of and work on the underlying cause, not on the symptom; accept your limitations—if you do less well in one type of skill, try something else; develop your potentialities—keep learning new things and be patient with yourself as you learn; be willing to assume responsibility—tackle that tough job and do your best! Don't expect the impossible of yourself—and don't compare yourself to the fellow next door!

Your prejudices. You aren't born with your prejudices; they are learned, like all behavior. A song from the musical *South Pacific* says "You have to be carefully taught" your prejudices. You certainly do! By the time children enter school, most have deeply rooted prejudices which probably develop like this: when a child is unhappy, feels unwanted or unappreciated—and don't we all, at times!—he cannot vent his unhappiness and resulting feelings of hostility on his family or his friends. He may *feel* that they have failed him, yet he depends on them for affection and recognition. However, he can—without fear of reprisal—vent his feelings on certain other people.

Who the certain people are depends partly on the part of the country in which he lives, on his parents' economic status, on their religious and political beliefs. His "hates" are usually channeled into his parents' "pet peeves": the Catholics, Protestants or Jews, Irish, Chinese, Italians, Mexicans, Japanese, Negroes or Whites, Republicans or Democrats, unions, big business, farmers, or the government.

Examining the origin of your prejudices can help you to understand that, often you don't really "think that way." You have, however, *learned* to feel that way. Combating prejudice is difficult largely because understanding the origin of prejudice means admitting to yourself your anxiety and hostility. It is unpleasant to face the fact that one projected onto someone else, or onto some group of people, one's own grievance, fear, or hostility. One's pride is wounded when one finds that he resorted to a scapegoat to avoid facing his own problems. Everyone likes to think of himself as a right-thinking, well-adjusted, generous person! Of course, one's picture of oneself may be somewhat rosy— but it is the best one has!

Moreover, it is disturbing to reveal the anxiety which prejudice effectively concealed. Perhaps one had convinced oneself that one's feelings were well-founded; you or your family actually had "gotten a raw deal" from the people you hate! Now, as one examines with honesty the origin of prejudice, one may be on the brink of discovering that what one had blamed on others may represent a weakness, or a fault, in oneself or one's family. In this crisis of feelings, it is difficult to take stock of oneself. The more important it is for a person to be "right," the more false pride is involved in one's need to blame others rather than to grow in responsibility oneself, the more threatening and painful this experience will be.

Can you pay the price of examining your particular prejudices? Apply the paragraphs above to yourself. Then, with an open mind, begin learning something about people or situations in which you have been blindly prejudiced. Take advantage of opportunities in your school, campus, job, church and community groups to become familiar with people and situations new to you, ones which you, without thinking, had termed "strange, different, sinister."

Observe the effects of prejudice and discrimination—how would you feel if you were rejected or isolated because of something you couldn't help, like your nationality or the color of your skin? Yet you want to make another human being feel like that? "Put yourself in their shoes"—this ability is the supreme secret of successful relationships with people!

You need to try yourself out with people. You and your feelings interact with other people and their feelings. No one, however, can see or understand *all* that is happening in his relationships with other people. Unconsciously, everyone is selective in what he sees and in the way he interprets his observation. A person recognizes, understands, remembers, repeats, and acts according to what is important to him. He is oblivious to all else.

Suppose that you were describing a club meeting in which the president had clumsily snubbed one of the members. If you were a "backer" of the president, organizer of the group which elected him, and felt somewhat responsible for his actions, or were perhaps the beneficiary of favors from him, you obviously would describe the incident differently from the way in which it would be described by the person who was snubbed. What each of you saw is probably different from what the president saw.

Personal biases are both normal and universal. Everyone brings to human relationships a variety of feelings about others and about himself. Your observation of anyone's behavior is colored by what you feel and believe about that particular person.

It is fascinating to try to teach yourself to observe so as to become *aware* of differences between you and other people, yet not to feel compelled to judge them, or to be afraid of them, or annoyed by them. If teenagers learn to concentrate on what other people are *actually* saying and doing, they will learn that the same behavior does not mean the

137

same thing to all people. There are *other* ways of viewing and interpreting behavior from the one you had accepted as *the* way.

You need, therefore, to face *your* biases if you are to look at people and situations without too much distortion. Ask yourself, "What did I actually see—what did this person actually say and do? To what extent am I imposing my ideas, judgments, or prejudices on the situation as I describe it?" Don't expect yourself to be impartial or without feelings. This would mean that you have no sensitivity, no values, no frame of reference. Don't try to eliminate these—but recognize them, make them explicit and clear to yourself and to those people with whom you are discussing something or someone. In other words, explain your point of view, "This is what I think he or she did—but I like her or him—I'd give them the benefit of the doubt" or "I'm afraid I'd expect him to act that way. I think he hasn't had enough experience to face that situation."

Your point of view *is* different. In fact, you *are* so different from anyone else that you couldn't possibly *be* anyone else. Everyone assumes this difference; it is the starting point in any new relationship. You have to "be yourself" in order to see yourself apart from the crowd—and to know yourself a person who has something to offer another.

You need to try yourself out with groups. Only as teen-agers have experiences in working with, playing with, and being with many widely differing groups of people can they learn to share, to cooperate, to listen to and confer with others, to respect and accept differences, to participate in and abide by group decisions—even when these do not incorporate their pet ideas!

138

What a teenager learns from any *one* group depends on the degree to which he feels himself a part of the group. For example, in a class at school, one teenager may seem lacking in energy, uninterested or slow, afraid to talk, unable to do assigned work. Although physically a part of this group, actually he participates in it to a minimal degree. On an athletic team, the same person may be a dynamo, an organizer, a coach in skills in which others are far clumsier and less advanced than he. Obviously, the skills and attitudes he develops in these two situations differ.

Another teenager may, in his family group, be quiet, well-behaved, self-contained; yet, at school, the group considers him a clown. On the other hand, the clown, in another situation—on the baseball field or on a camping trip—may be so absorbed in what he is seeing, hearing, or doing that the quality of his participation in this group has a genuineness not found in the conformist behavior he uses at home or the attention-getting behavior he resorts to in school.

In the last-mentioned group, the teenager was neither forced into a pattern nor did he disguise himself by clowning. His interest was aroused; his latent capacities challenged; his basic needs met. Regardless of how one may judge his behavior, plainly the same teenager is learning a variety of abilities and attitudes because of the range of experiences he gains in each group.

To develop an increasing number of your potentialities, become absorbed in numerous group activities which demand sustained attention. Thus, you grow continuously in self-discipline, self-criticism, ability to accept criticism from others, and ability to express yourself in a variety of materials—to develop ideas verbally or to embody them in music, in a blueprint, a piece of furniture, a clay figure, a new farm product, a steak dinner, or whatever becomes your individualized way of contributing to a given group's activities.

Such learning is different from conforming to set rules, from copying examples or models, from memorizing facts or giving correct answers. Those teenagers who are able only to talk and to write use just a segment of their ability. Striving for excellence in narrowly "academic" areas alone may actually disguise a lack of genuine *knowing how* to relate to people and things. Through *many* group experiences, you discover that your assets are greater and more numerous than you had suspected. As you dig up and use your assets, you learn to express and develop your "self."

You and Your Date

THIS IS your "enchanted evening"! You see your "stranger across the crowded room." You meet him or her—and dance. Each thinks the other a "heavenly" dancer! You go walking, and as he touches your shoulder to place your coat around you, you both shiver. Together you look at the moon on the lake—and catch your breath. You begin to

141

dream of lifelong romance. Already you hear the magic words, "Will you marry me?" Everyone dreams either of saying them or hearing them said.

Everyone date-dreams! A basic occupation of every teen-ager is looking for the kind of person he or she might marry. The search begins early; the median age when girls make a decision to marry has, in our country, dropped to 20.2 years! Is it surprising, then, that in your teens you clearly envision this chosen one?

What's he like—tall, brown eyes, well-built or brawny, brown crewcut or medium-long black hair? Is she five feet five, slim, a blonde with wavy hair, blue eyes, a neat dresser? You're sure you'd recognize him or her at first glance!

What is he or she like on the inside? Studies of what teenagers expect in a life partner emphasize that, above all, he be a good provider. Maybe he's a business executive, a pilot, an engineer, or a doctor. He's not rude; he's not stingy; he's not bossy; he's not possessive. He wants a large family; he likes to go out and have fun. She's loving; she's interested in him above everything; she's sympathetic; she's responsive sexually and true to him; she's a good mother to his family; she's careful with his money; she's a good hostess —an attractive person whom he enjoys showing off to his friends. Oh, that's the person you could love!! So when you meet him or her on this "enchanted" evening—and you've recognized one another as your dream come true, are you in love?

In our country, unrealistic romance is overemphasized; real love is not always understood. The movies, radio, tele-vision, and slick magazines seem to say to girls: If you want to be loved, be beautiful—or smell good: "she's lovely—she's

142

engaged—she uses" this or that face cream, soap, or deodorant. A boy is told that, if he does not use this hair tonic for dandruff, or that shaving cream—if he is not handsome and fragrant, girls will not love him!

The story goes on with false notions: if you use this nail polish or that shampoo, you will "get your man" or woman and you will marry. If you marry, you will be happy. However, as you examine the advertisements closely, do the average teenagers—*as you know them*—look like, dress like, or act like those pictured greeting one another in luxurious homes with ultramodern décor—or helping ermine-clad women into expensive automobiles?

Would the "beautiful doll" you envision or the "perfect catch" of whom you dream give you, as you are today, a second look? Do you murmur reluctantly, and only to yourself, "I wonder?" Quickly, you add wistfully, "But I can dream, can't I?" By all means! There is a type of dreaming which can add solid planks to a platform on which to build a permanent relationship. For example, instead of working on *finding* a mythical companion and partner, work on how you can *become* such a person.

So He's the Perfect Date—But Is It Love?

Actually, preparation for dating as well as marriage began almost on the day of your birth! All your years of growth and development you have become, and are still becoming, the kind of person who will or will not make a good companion, a good husband and father, wife and mother. Some of you may already be prizes. Others, unless you do something about yourselves, will be poor date material now and difficult to live with later—your partners may not be able to "take it"! What's *your* sales value—to borrow a term from the ads!

What do you look like? Have you learned that, by "looks," people do not mean physical beauty, but the attractiveness that comes from being self-confident—poised, interested in everyone, and in all that goes on round you; having a ready smile, head held high, good posture; being well-groomed with that fresh and spotless look, poor features disguised or made the most of, and clothes worn with the expectation of being looked at with approval?

Your "date" has asked, "What are we doing tomorrow?" What *can* you do? Are you a good swimmer, skier, skater, bowler, camper, dancer, tennis player, musician, fisherman, conversationalist? If not, are you willing to learn—or do you like only television? It's so easy just to sit and look. What interests you? If you are to carry a *two-way* conversation, both of you need to know about cars, politics, people, sports, gardening, electronics—even atoms!

What kind of person are you? Are you honestly interested in your date? Can you make him or her feel that his hobbies are important to you, that you want to hear about his or her last vacation, first memory, or new "boss"? Do you listen to him or her—or just wait for a pause, then crowd your life history into your first half hour together? Do you try to learn something from your date? Can you admit "I don't know" because you honestly want information he or she can give you?

Can you show appreciation or compliment him or her with poise? If he or she compliments you, do you thank your date graciously or do you laugh or ridicule with remarks like: "Are you blind or something?"—or—"Bet you tell that

144

to everybody"? Are you thoughtful and imaginative in planning what you do together, or do you haphazardly settle for movies and a soda? If you "can't think of anything new to suggest," he or she apparently is not important enough to warrant the effort of thinking.

Are you adaptable enough to enjoy, for example, getting caught in the rain if you are on a picnic? Can you think of something else quickly when you both feel let down because, on your arrival, you find a "Closed Monday" sign on that "swell place to eat" he'd bragged about? He feels such a "dope"; do you show by word or facial expression that you're inclined to agree? It is very important for two people to know how to handle situations involving the self-respect of either one.

Can you express your pleasure in one another's company with an understanding smile, a touch of the hand, a repetition of a remark of the other person's which you'd obviously tucked away to remember, or a request for something he or she can do which can be of genuine help to you? In other words, can you show admiration and respect for a person by treating him or her as an *individual,* not as just another date?

What is the judgment of your peers? Are you popular because you like other people and are interested in the things they are? What is your reputation among the opposite sex—are you cool, smooth, fun to be with, a good sport, a dope, a wolf, a wet blanket, fast, or cheap? Do you have standards you believe in not because "the crowd" says you must, but because you know what kind of man or woman you want to become? Can you treasure your standards— but not preach them?

You may not yet have developed a sense of direction to guide your day-by-day actions. If you have too little self-confidence, your behavior may be controlled by your fear of teasing or of sarcasm from the gang or from your family. Particularly if you are in a new school, job, or community—or if friendship with the opposite sex is a relatively new experience, you may pretend a sophistication you do not feel, perhaps experiment with some of the "crowd's" behavior patterns in which you are not really comfortable; unquestioningly you may follow the dictates of the gang or ape the behavior of those of your friends who seem, outwardly at least, popular with the opposite sex.

As, gradually, you gain respect for the person you are, you begin to visualize the kind of person you want to be. Because you wish to become a person someone will want to live with for years and years, you face the cause-and-effect relationship of your daily behavior: "If I do this tonight, will it help or hinder me in becoming the kind of person I want to be five years from now?"

Thus you grow toward maturity. But are you ready for love? "Being a swell date" does not, in itself, mean that you can meet the demands and responsibilities of love. Regardless of anyone's chronological age, love is not a sudden, overpowering emotion which takes hold of two people when "boy meets girl." Two people can love only if both are capable of love.

What Is Love?

What is love—really? Something mysterious that just happens to you—or doesn't? Does one go around looking for love—outside oneself? Some people think so. They believe that *to love* is simple but that, in this world of ours, *to be loved* is difficult. Quite the contrary is true. You are loved only if you can love—if your capacity to love produces love in another person. Immature people, primarily concerned about whether they will be loved, ask in every relationship, "What can I get out of this?" rather than "What can I put in?" The real problem is not the difficulty of being loved, but the difficulty of *loving*. Have you grown far enough away from self-centeredness to be able truly to care about someone else?

There is no more fundamental force in humanity than the craving for love. In infancy and childhood, the actual, physical need for love originates in helplessness; an infant and child must *be* loved. His very "life depends on it." However, "by adult life one *can* be strong enough to develop the enjoyment of *loving* others." *

"When the satisfaction and security of another person becomes as significant to one as is one's own satisfaction or security, then the state of love exists. So far as I know, under no other circumstances is a state of love present, regardless of the popular usage of the word." † *The Hit Parade*, Hollywood, soap operas, charm magazines, cold cream, deodorant and hair-oil ads to the contrary notwithstanding!

Have you ever thought about whether *you* can love anyone but yourself? Have you developed the *capacity to love* which *produces* love in another person? Capacity to love *should* develop as you pass through various stages from in-

* Leon Saul, *Emotional Maturity*, J. B. Lippincott, Philadelphia, 1947, p. 114.

† Henry S. Sullivan, *Conceptions of Modern Psychiatry*, W. A. White Psychiatric Foundation, Washington, D.C., 1941, p. 20.

fancy to adulthood. Young children may be fond of or like their parents or other people; but, until a child has grown into self-awareness enough to see others as different from himself, he cannot give to others—he can only take. He takes all the love and care so necessary to his life. A young child cannot respond to emotional demands or to human needs; he spends his time happily with inanimate objects—toys and dolls—which make no demands on him. *Self-centeredness and love for someone else cannot go together; to be "free" to love, one must grow away from childish self-centeredness.*

A child's first step toward capacity to love may be a live pet who needs him and is dependent on him—or a younger brother or sister for whom he feels genuine responsibility. Mature teenagers speak with pride of younger brothers and sisters "needing" their help. Being needed is a maturing experience; it teaches you how to give—thereby it develops capacity to love another as yourself.

A child's first experience in *freely choosing* to give love came when he or she chose his first friend. It was an atmosphere quite new to him—"friendship in its first stage when one is giving all—not yet having discovered either how much it is vain to offer or expect—a first slight bridge, a wavering feeler out of the shell of self." *

A child's first friend is a person of his own sex because, generally, in our culture before adolescence boys scorn girls and girls consider boys nasty or sloppy. Remember, however, that when such taunts are directed too often at a particular boy or girl, they are, in reality, the beginnings of in-

* Sean O'Faolain, *Bird Alone*, The Viking Press, Inc., New York, 1936, p. 242.

terest in the opposite sex! As a boy or girl grows physically, his feelings and attitudes toward the opposite sex change from contempt to interest.

Teen-age boys and girls *try* to understand one another and to express feelings to one another. Naturally, they are clumsy and inept at first, as we all are at any skill new to us. Failure "to get across" plunges them into despair. However, as they keep trying, a sense of companionship with the opposite sex develops. Then dating becomes, not just filling up a calendar to prove that one is popular, but experience in what it feels like to give and take, freely to choose and be chosen. Everyone grows in emotional maturity through the experience of being wanted, finding that he or she is desirable—or desired—and has something to give to someone else.

Whether or not two young people who enjoy "dating" one another and being together will be capable of loving one another depends on the degree to which each has developed capacity to give and receive. This, in turn, is dependent on whether each sufficiently accepts and respects *himself*.

Love or self-centeredness. Capacity to love may be blocked at infantile or childish levels. In infancy, when parents' care is necessary for actual survival, "love" has a desperate, clinging quality. Young children—some teenagers and some adults—retain these attitudes, feelings, and habits. The clinging, demanding type of attachment betrays such a teenager; he is concerned primarily about his *own* feelings. A great *need* for love motivates this self-absorbed person desperately to seek love.

Teenagers like this are not self-centered because they

care only about *themselves*. They are incapable of loving *anyone*, including themselves. They are self-absorbed because they are so worried about themselves—they consider themselves of so little value that they cannot imagine anyone valuing them. They cannot reach out to others because they think they have nothing to give. Although their need to be loved is much stronger than a mature teenager's need, their fears and insecurities cause them to behave in a way that robs them of what they most desire.

Emotional immaturity, in its various forms, is the greatest single threat to success in love and marriage. For example, a self-centered individual—be he fifteen or fifty—never grows beyond the stage of infatuation. For a person with a deep feeling of inadequacy to find that someone loves him —that he *is* lovable—produces tremendous emotion. He overreacts; he is infatuated.

Because he needs love so much, a person like this can be victimized by any individual who pretends a reasonable facsimile of love. On the other hand, the infatuated person, though superficially concerned about his partner, is concerned mainly with the feeling of worth his partner can give him. A self-centered person is perpetually seeking in another what he must first find in himself.

You have seen the kind of adult who cannot keep up any relationship—who always has to "break it off." When a partner cannot satisfy his extravagant demands, as no one can, the self-centered person blames the partner for withholding something he wants and needs—"he or she—let me down!" One can learn, from adolescent infatuations, that one had no reason to expect more love than one was able to give.

150

Another type of self-centered individual is one who carefully measures what others give him before he begins to give. Perhaps he was expected by his parents to love them as repayment for their "care and sacrifices" for him. Love to him, therefore, has nothing to do with accepting and valuing himself and his development—or the other person's. He bargains or demands because he thinks that people receive love in proportion to their sacrifices—or even their needs—not in proportion to their capacity to love—or to be lovable!

A self-centered person sees love only as a means of satisfying personal desires. Although he or she may feel attracted to one individual after another, no relationship differs essentially from any other because this immature person cannot feel deeply for anyone. He cannot give freely; he is too interested in what he will get.

When it's love, you're not looking for personal satisfaction alone; you're not picking a person as you would new clothes —for what they'll do to enhance you! True, some teenagers *seem* to do so. Some even seem to marry calculatingly, perhaps for money or social prestige. Such a person's dearest wish seems to be to have his—or her—marriage labeled "successful" or to have life made easier because of financial security or acceptance by a certain social group!

When either partner's desire to be "taken care of" is the dominant aim in a relationship, the resulting marriage is on a precarious basis. Such a person is not ready for a mature relationship; he merely desires padding against the outside world. Therefore, he or she seeks a wife or husband who will pamper and indulge him as did a mother, father, or intimate friend. On the other hand, this type of person may shy away from marriage because he or she cannot bear to leave his comfortable home with his mother's absorbed devotion or his father's affection and protection.

Some self-centered people confuse their feelings. A young man may say that he does not want to give up his freedom or that he does not have the money to marry, when what he really means is that he cannot bear to leave his mother. Perhaps a young woman says that she wants a career instead of marriage or that she could not lower her standard of living for a man—when really she still idealizes her father and is seeking someone like him. Should she find him, she will treat him like her father; she cannot think of herself as a woman in relation to him as a man. Some adults actually are so dependent emotionally on their parents that they are unable to live away from them.

Other self-centered people would rather have money, clothes, expensive cars, and world cruises than marriage! If taking and spending are more important than giving or sharing, a person is too immature to love. What of the young man or woman who says that his or her job is the all-important factor in life, that he needs nothing else? Actually, if he or she faced himself honestly, he might find that he is not yet ready to love anyone as much as himself.

Some teenagers are "so afraid" that people, particularly of the opposite sex, do not like them! The real problem with a person like this is that he does not consider *himself* likable, therefore believes that no one could care about him. He may have within himself the feeling that he is not the kind of person he ought to be. This lack of self-respect may be so deep that he has neither realized it nor acknowledged it.

If a teenager clings to the idea that he cannot do something and acts as though it were futile to try, the next step naturally follows. He *feels* inadequate. When he loses a friend or a date, he thinks it is because he is incapable of holding friends or does not "deserve" them. Such a teen-ager needs to grow up—to face his fears and insecurities, develop his interests and abilities, and create for himself opportunities to meet and enjoy people.

During this process, an insecure teenager may venture only a short distance into this strange new world of the other sex, then cling desperately to the first person who makes him feel secure because this person shows him that he is liked. People of all ages have experiences like this. Some young people marry the first person available to prove to themselves that they are marriageable—or because all the gang is getting married. They say that they "don't know anyone else" so they'd better marry someone in the gang! Some adults hastily marry someone "on the rebound." Such an insecure person thinks he is "in love" with his "catch." Actually, she is the first kind or reassuring person to consider him attractive after he has lived through some unfortunate experience with a woman. Insecure people, shrinking from the possibility of being hurt again, cling to any semblance of understanding and security.

The younger you are or the more inclined you are to be a one-man woman or a one-woman man, the more likely you are to "grab" for and date the first available person, then fancy that you have fallen in love. What a teenager mistakes for love may actually be the security and prestige of being "date material," the thrill of being attractive to and chosen by someone, the gratification of having someone to count on; or perhaps it is simply relief at no longer having to "wait around for someone to telephone"; the fact that a particular individual makes you feel comfortable—especially if making friends with the opposite sex is, for some reason, not easy for you; or it is the desire to possess this particular individual so that you can prove to yourself and others that you *are* attractive to the opposite sex. The latter is especially pertinent if your prize happens to be the May Day Queen, the Boss's daughter, or the captain of the football team!

Your first or second boyfriend or girl friend—even your first or second "big romance"—is not necessarily the person with whom you can live happily for the rest of your life. Neither of you may be ready for love or marriage. The mature teenagers who say that they do not want to marry "in a hurry" imply knowledge of this fact. They may be deeply wounded when a "first love" is terminated; but they are not panic-stricken. They know that they are *more* capable of loving because they have learned something of the joys and frustrations, the responsibilities and limitations of a real give-and-take relationship.

They have also learned something of their own and of another person's needs and expectations. They will, therefore, be more selective in their choice of possible mates; they are less likely to choose individuals whose personality will clash with theirs. They will be guided by increased realism as well as strong personal attraction in choosing, and, later, living with their life partner.

To feel that one must "hang on" to the first individual to whom one is attracted physically also betrays lack of confidence in oneself. If a teenager knows that he or she is

154

attractive, that he likes people and is liked by them, he or she undoubtedly will, sometime during life, feel "that way" again about someone and have that someone respond! Immaturity and inexperience sometimes cause teenagers to mistake physical attraction for love. Physical attraction is important; it must be present if a relationship is to be permanent. But love is not exclusively nor even primarily physical. A lasting relationship cannot, therefore, be built on physical attraction alone.

How does anyone know that he or she may not, after marriage, "feel that way" about some other person? It is possible, throughout life, for one to feel attracted to many individuals consecutively or at the same time. Whether or not he or she "responds" to someone depends upon such factors as: how much one desires the companionship of the opposite sex at the moment one meets, how free or occupied one's mind is with other concerns, how rested or tired one is, or how great one's range of choice is. If you haven't had many dates and he or she chooses *you*, you may think it's romance—even after you're married!

Every teenager must be certain that he has given the other "date material" sufficient consideration so that, if he decides to marry someone, he does not keep, back in his mind, a doubt that he might have made a better choice. This is a possibility. However, if by the time he meets another person with whom he might have been happy, he has —in a mature, thoughtful manner—chosen someone else and achieved a vital, satisfactory marriage relationship, then the second person becomes merely another of a group of friends whom he finds interesting. There is no intimate place for her to occupy. Being "realistic" about an attraction means accepting the responsibility involved in loving. Loving without thinking is blatant immaturity.

A teenager who has clung to one person cannot escape wondering "do I love him or am I only accustomed to him?" Suppose, however, that you have known many young people, then have chosen one. If, during a long acquaintance, each becomes "accustomed" to the other, in the sense of adjusting gradually, becoming accustomed to each other is good. In the give-and-take of real love, each person will change or adjust. He cannot *be* changed; he must change himself. Since change is often painful, no one will change unless he or she *wants* to change. One must care a great deal about another person to want to change. Genuine change—or adjustment—will, therefore, be the result of a mutual, voluntary, realistic appraisal of oneself and the other person.

Genuine love cannot be commanded because of another's need or sacrifice—or demanded out of fear or threat of punishment. Capacity to love presupposes freedom. To "love" someone because of the accident of family relationship, or because one is not free to love someone else, or because one cannot do without the other person is sham and hypocrisy.

Mature love manifests itself in deep pleasure in another person whose "self" you accept—*as it is*—and whose development you value as you do your own. In mature love, you lose—and find—yourself in concern about someone else. As you voluntarily tie up your life with that of another, you are freed of yourself. However, you can release and merge yourself only if you have a "self" to give. Unless you are certain that you have a "self" which can stand alone, you will hold yourself back because you fear losing your identity.

Actually, you do not lose your "self" in love; on the contrary, in the highest expression of love, you fulfill your "self." A voluntary yielding in and to love can transform the immature *will to want* into the *will to be wanted*. It, in turn, becomes the desire to give. Mature love is *freely* giving one's "self"; it is not forced giving-up or abdicating one's "self," nor is it a forced holding-on. You feel *union with*, not triumph over, another person as you fulfill your love. You give yourself and find yourself at once—a new "self" because wanted by, accepted by, and incorporated with the other. This is mature love. It is far too rare because it is difficult to learn. And, because it is rare, you need to recognize other emotions, masquerading as love, for what they are.

The One "Meant for You"

You may conclude, correctly, that there is no one "right" person for you. Love, in all its aspects, does not "fall" upon you suddenly, full-blown. It develops slowly. If you become an attractive person, if you enjoy and reach out toward other people, inevitably people will respond to you. You, in turn, will begin to choose "special" people—and finally someone!

Suppose you think that you have found a person "meant for you," how can you assure yourself that "this will last"? If you both know that you are attracted to each other; if you can enter marriage physically, mentally, and emotionally fit; if you both honestly attempt to become continuously more mature emotionally; if you have intelligently estimated the possibilities of making your marriage a constantly growing partnership; if you understand the obligations as well as the joys of marriage; if you feel that there is mutual loyalty and genuine comradeship between you, that, in fact, you each achieve, in the other person, completion of yourself, then you have all the certainty anyone can ever know!

What considerations will help you to decide whether you can answer in the affirmative the questions implied above? In marriage, two people need to live in a multiple relationship with each other; they must be able to share many aspects of life. Sometimes, two people may be suited to play together and entertain each other during their teens—this does not necessarily mean that they can live together for a lifetime.

Similar goals. What growth do you each expect of the other as you envision the relationship you both will create? Can the two of you learn to manage a home together? Can you cooperate on a standard of living even if it is different from the one to which you have been accustomed? Can you work out a budget and "make it stick"? Do you both have constructive attitudes toward sex and toward working out a happy mutual relationship? Can you cooperate in planning for and rearing children? Can you understand and respect each other's attitudes on the status of the woman and her interests outside the home, on the man's responsibilities in the house, on religion or the values in life you each are seeking?

Sufficient similar characteristics and interests. It is sometimes true that opposite characteristics contribute to a happy adjustment; but there must also be sufficient in common between two people to make a day-by-day relationship possible. For example, a methodical, matter-of-fact husband may be troubled by the household disorder of a wife who
158

prefers to spend her time in aesthetic pursuits, while she may consider her husband uncultured and interested only in money. If one partner is too much the intellectual superior of the other, or if one revels in parties and entertaining while the other feels uncomfortable in social gatherings, there may be difficulty in working out happy adjustments.

On the other hand, if two young people have common interests in too narrow a sphere, their relationship may also be endangered. Two people who excel in the same sport or work in the same profession need to take care that they do not become competitors.

A relationship must be strong to survive constant association. Young people need some continuing basis for conversation. You need to do many things together: work and play—sharing tasks in and for your home, learning new skills and leisure-time pursuits. Can each multiply the interests of the other? Do you have friends in common? Does each enjoy the other's friends? Friends are especially important if one is marrying someone outside his social group, religion, or nationality, when one may temporarily be shunned by the family group.

Sufficient emotional maturity. Are both of you emotionally mature enough for a permanent relationship? Like the unrealistic presentation of love in our culture, marriage is presented, in too much fiction, advertising, and movies, through the rosy glow of "lifelong romance." A good marriage becomes *that*, through mature and realistic love—and work—but not through emphasis on ranch houses, streamlined kitchens, and tables set with sterling silver.

Marriage is not accompanied by a gilt-edged certificate guaranteeing that you will live happily ever after—except in a dream world! Successful marriage takes place in a real world. Its goal is genuine happiness, not unrealistic romance. Only the immature believe the fairy tales which end: "They were married and lived happily ever after"—apparently without effort on *their* part!

Unfortunately, some immaturity is a product of the emphasis in our country on giving teenagers a "carefree youth." Youth is prized as "the best time in your life." Parents, inclined to lament teenagers' growing up, sometimes "excuse them" as long as possible from "responsibilities." By depriving them of helping in the home, they rob them of training in facing the problems of a homemaker. No matter what the state of the husband's pocketbook or how many labor-saving devices they own, a young couple still must buy and cook food, clean and manage a home, and bring up children—and they need to know how!

Emotionally mature behavior is behavior appropriate to the situation. Suppose an eighteen- or nineteen-year-old woman with a responsible job and good salary is "going steady" with a young man who is preparing for a profession. She thinks that she wants to marry him until she discovers that he must continue his schooling for several years after their marriage. In a tantrum, she angrily states that she will marry no man to support him. She is not ready for the responsibility of marriage if she expects that a man will give up, for her, his training in a highly competitive professional field where advanced education is necessary for even moderate financial success. Modern marriage often necessitates the wife's working outside the home—for a time at least.

Or, perhaps a couple has decided to marry just before a young man goes into the service. Can they honestly and thoughtfully consider several alternatives such as: living in crowded, possibly unsatisfactory quarters in some barracks town or the young woman's remaining home and continuing in her job? If they decide on the latter, can they both learn to "fill up" lonely evenings and still remain true to one another? Of course, they probably won't plan on a baby—lots of young people don't; then they have one. Have they discussed this possibility with both sets of parents—if she is to remain at home while he is away?

Will they be grownup in this discussion with the parents—or will they push baby off onto grandma? One young couple explained, "Stan and I agreed that I'd stay home and take care of the baby—and we'd pay my parents his allotment for our keep until Stan got out of the service." She admitted it wasn't easy to bring up an infant with constant "good advice" from grandparents. But she managed. She and her husband had, consciously and maturely, made a choice—and were willing to abide by its consequences.

This is not the kind of couple likely to have a scene over household bills. The wife will not petulantly insist upon a new dress or the husband upon a new car when the oil bill has to be paid. One will not state categorically, "We can't take on any more right now," while the other hurls reproaches of "You don't love me"—the implication being "or you'd give me what I want when I want it"! Such young people are acting like infants.

At what age shall you marry? If you can face daily problems maturely, you are answering the question—at what age shall I marry? Today's couple is ready to marry when both are emotionally mature enough to understand the meaning and fulfill the obligations of marriage as it must be worked out today. Marriage is a complicated undertaking. All the responsibilities formerly connected with homemaking and child-rearing are required of modern young couples— plus some new ones such as: more education than was necessary even ten years ago; vocational skills which will make it possible for both partners, if necessary, to be wage earners; willingness, when this is essential, to establish a home far from parents and friends and to run it well, generally without household help.

No neat formula, especially not one which considers chronological age alone, can determine the "best" age to marry! The 1950 census shows that while in 1890 the median age of young men at the time of their first marriage was 26.7, in 1950 it was 22.5 years. The women's median age was 22, now it is 20.2 years. Not too long ago, women— and some men—were expelled from college if they married. Now, many colleges are building garden apartments for married students and their families.

Families? Young people are having babies earlier—and closer together; closer together because they say that they do not want two or more "only" children growing up years apart; earlier, apparently, because of several factors: during prosperity, we dare to invest in a future; depressions delay marriages. Moreover, most young people have attitudes toward financial responsibility and toward living standards different from those of the previous generation.

In these days, when education for highly skilled occupations and for the professions is prolonged, when military service interrupts study and work, many young people feel that they cannot wait to have families until they are financially established. Many parents so sincerely encourage

162

early marriages and child rearing that they eagerly help young people financially in order that young people may begin their families. In fact, some parents help too much—and some young people expect too much!

When some young people marry today, both accept the possibility that each may work to keep their home going. Both do the work they are trained to do outside the home; then each partner helps inside the home with feeding the family, housekeeping, and baby care. Other couples may decide that the wife will remain at home with the children. These young women, who have probably held "good jobs," realize that marriage will be anything but easy when babies come close together and they must learn to get along on one skimpy budget instead of two—often without relatives or paid help, without reserve of funds or of energy for emergencies. Nevertheless, they *choose* husbands, babies, and family life rather than material goods and high living standards. Mature love is the abiding motive of these marriages.

You and Your Marriage

"WHAT ON EARTH does he see in her?—or she in him?"
You've probably heard and used this expression. What will
someone see in you? Suppose you apply to yourself what
you looked for in the "one meant for you." How will you

164

learn what you need to know? How will you get along with him—or her—and his friends?

What Kind of Marriage Partner Will You Be?

You will be, on your wedding morning, exactly the kind of person you are making yourself now. You did not wake up some morning knowing how to ride a bicycle, play the piano, drive a car, wear your clothes well—or even how to be a pleasant person. You cannot expect to wake up on your wedding morning knowing how to be a good companion, a good husband and father, or wife and mother, unless you are, daily, learning the necessary skills and attitudes.

What are you like today? Do you meet people easily and accept new friends eagerly? Are you willing to share privileges, possessions—and your friends? Do you help when there is work to do? Are you as cooperative in carrying out other people's plans as you expect them to be in carrying out your desires? Are you generally pleasant, resourceful, and unselfish? Or are you inclined to become stubborn and unreasonable when you don't get your way?

Can you talk out your difficulties with people rationally; can you compromise where necessary without resentment? Can you make decisions cooperatively with someone else, or must the other person always give in while you get your way? Marriage won't change you from what you are now. It is not as easy, sometimes, to *be* the right person as it was to *find* the right person to marry!

In marriage, you will need to know how to face disappointments, perhaps heavy responsibilities and financial setbacks, with faith in the other person intact. This will not be easy. Will you understand that husbands and wives, in the happiest marriages, each wonder at times whether they really love their spouses, whether their spouses love them, and whether they are worthy of the love?

What do you know about managing a home? Is it necessary to train to be a homemaker, some of you may ask? Interestingly enough, you accept the fact that you need training to be a waitress, to operate a machine in a factory, to be a nurse, a stenographer, or a cab driver. Do you assume that you can enter the most important job of your life without training?

What is partnership? You need to understand that marriage today demands that the "good" husband or wife be a different sort of person from the previous generation's concept. There is no longer a sharp distinction of function between husband and wife. The woman's sphere today is similar to the man's—in law and in conditions of everyday economic life. For example, the wife may earn half or even all the family income; she may earn nothing this year but decide to work next.

The successful husband and father-to-be is the one who has forgotten about traditional rights and prerogatives of a lord and master. He is a man living under the same roof with a loved woman in an atmosphere of give-and-take, gay and warm affection, and shared work—one who does not wish to be released from joint responsibility for the firm's success!

On the other hand, the woman needs to feel that her most important career and greatest source of pride is in ensuring the happiness of her husband and children. She tries day by day to give her husband the security that she *believes* in their marriage and in him. Her home means more to her than a house with a washer, ironer, freezer, and television set; her husband more than a free escort and entertainment service. They are two people working together, making a home and building a family, each deeply content in his contribution to the common enterprise.

Marriage is a contract in which each partner must fulfill his obligation. Marriage is for grown-up people—people mature enough to deal with situations and problems in terms of fact, not emotion. Every young couple, undoubtedly, will lack experience in some situations and some problems, but if each partner has prepared himself by anticipating as many situations as possible and has gained skill in meeting a variety of problems, then both together will possess the courage to face new experiences and to seek intelligent solutions.

If You Want a Happy Marriage

"Living happily ever after" is the coveted goal. After the rice has washed into the gutter and the wedding silver begins to tarnish, the most serious and soul-trying, as well as the most thrilling part of your married life begins. Marriage holds both promise and danger. It is a relationship in which the weaknesses of your personality are discovered and the strengths rewarded.

Its promise is that marriage can be a haven wherein both partners can achieve adequacy and gain the warm, security-giving satisfactions which everyone needs. To fulfill this promise, each must, however, have sufficient emotional maturity to make further maturing possible. If a couple cannot grow, marriage is a cage wherein more hatred, fear, and resentment can be generated than in any other human relationship.

Look outside yourself. If you have chosen your partner wisely, you will begin this long, exciting, and sometimes painful period of growing toward further maturity without fear. Neither of you will be discouraged by initial awkwardness or trial-and-error behavior of the other. With so much emotion and so many hopes invested in this marriage experience, it is not surprising if both act clumsily in the early days—it is like verbal clumsiness; just when one wants to say the right thing, one stumbles over words.

Gradually, two people striving for maturity learn how to give and how to receive one another's love. You discover that looking outside yourself and becoming concerned about the welfare of others—your spouse and your children—does not mean that you lose your "self" or that you value yourself less.

Unfortunately, some people fail to understand that you cannot receive love unless you are capable of giving. An immature person, upon entering marriage, is concerned primarily about his or her partner's ability to love him: Will I be appreciated? Will my love be reciprocated? rather than: Am *I* capable of loving him or her? If you look *into yourself* only, marriage is an invitation to watch your moods with tender solicitude and wonder whether or not you are happy.

You are especially prone to consider only yourself if you continue to go around with the dreamy, out-of-focus viewpoint of one "in love," the implication of this phrase being that you see the other person as something more than human.

168

Happiness and self-centeredness cannot exist together. If a person cannot give love, the marriage may end in divorce.

Welcome changes in yourself. Most teenagers are unaware of the fact that, in the give-and-take of a marriage relationship, each person changes frequently. You actually are a *different person* as a lover, a spouse, and a parent. Each new relationship makes you feel, act, and behave differently. This calls for flexibility. An immature person possesses little flexibility, therefore he will find it difficult to adapt to the demands of the many relationships to which marriage requires adjustment.

Some teen-age girls, for example, "glamor girls" or "popularity queens," may desire the prestige, romance, and security of marriage, but resent the marriage relationship when they find it changes their concerns from those centered on personal enhancement to the daily routine of running a home. With exaggerated ideas of their charms, they may feel unappreciated in a situation removed from the public eye. Some teen-age boys, accustomed to spending their money on themselves, may rebel when marriage changes them into the sole contributors to the household budget. Each marriage partner discovers, also, that the other is a different person from the courtship days. To face this truth may hurt; it is, nevertheless, a fact that, as most people live together in a day-by-day routine, each becomes less loving and more demanding.

In the happiest marriages, anger and resentments sometimes flare. If you know that these are due to tensions inevitable in intimate living together, you learn to deal with them with realism and without fear. Welcome changes as challenges. A marriage has maximum opportunity for success when both partners willingly try to tolerate realities emotionally and to build habits and attitudes suitable for dealing with them. For example, each willingly assumes responsibilities such as spending money, not for personal pleasure primarily, but for necessities of living and for underwriting future plans. Each learns to live with the fact that some daily chores must be shared. Each recognizes that his partner has a variety of responsibilities and cannot give the other his undivided attention. Each accepts the fact that every person needs some privacy.

However, an immature person may resist or evade change because he is upset and panicky lest he be unable to meet new responsibilities. Such a person may attempt to comfort himself, perhaps by arguing that marriage has changed nothing—"I'm going to live my life as I always did" or "I won't let my children tie me down"—or by immature wishing—"Things will get back to normal after the first year—or after we have a baby!"

When a partner is immature. When two self-centered people marry, life may become a series of skirmishes in which each tries to force the other to satisfy his demands. For example, two possessive people may require excessive attention or constant demonstrations of affection from one another, perhaps because they tried vainly to gain attention from indifferent parents—or from parents who showered all attention on a favored brother or sister. Each partner now becomes frantic if his or her spouse's attention is turned from him. He or she heaps on the partner sobbing recriminations that "You don't love me—or want me—or care whether I live or die." He or she may become ill, nagging, or jealous of the other's job, friends, hobby—even of the evening news-

170

paper or favorite television program! And woe be to the partner when he or she brings work home or when he or she "breaks a date" with his spouse because of business necessity!

On the other hand, an armed truce may develop in which one partner satisfies some of the other's demands in exchange for the satisfaction of some of his. If a wife or husband considers his contribution to a marriage to be money or social position, he or she may think of his partner, not as a person valuable in himself and with rights of his own, but as someone who, in exchange for money or social position, will accord him or her the constant, unquestioning devotion he craves—devotion which extends to his opinions as well as his physical and entertainment needs!

Another type of immaturity is the basis of the demand "I will be master here." A husband may, in making this demand, merely be copying the pattern to which he was accustomed in his own home. Or he may be resenting a too-dominant mother. Again, he may actually have enjoyed the overprotection given him by his mother, yet resented his dependence on her and despised himself for his weakness. Therefore, he now fights for position with all the bitterness of a person fighting his own nature.

A wife who is determined to "be boss in this family" may see her husband, not as a partner, but as a man—an enemy by whom she no longer will be dominated. She may have feared or envied her father and her brothers because they considered women weak or even contemptible. She may have identified with her mother, but hated this sense of weakness in herself—and now she is grimly determined to "be on top"! Should her husband yield—and he may if he actually desires a mother rather than a wife—she may despise him for the weakness she felt in herself; she may browbeat him; or, robbed of her adversary at home, she may bully people on her job—or in the community where she pours this energy into "good works."

Understand the role of sex in marriage. Many demands by both marriage partners arise in the area of sexual adjustment. An immature person wants to *"get"* sex satisfaction. He or she sees it as something he does not have and can secure only by *taking* it. Such a person may try to withhold it, if he or she wishes to punish or humiliate his partner or to extort favors. The mature person knows that sex satisfaction is not something which can be *taken from* one partner or the other. It is a *shared* experience, possible only if both partners know how to give and how to take.

The immature person expects too much of the sex act itself; the mature person knows that the sex act can be only one expression of the quality of an entire relationship. If a relationship is strained, unhappy, or lacking in mutual concern, sexual union will relieve momentary tensions, but cannot contribute to thoughtfulness and understanding. An immature person may blame his or her partner if sexual union does not give sex satisfaction at once. A mature person knows that it may take months, sometimes years, to achieve a sexual union satisfying to both husband and wife. Final achievement of satisfying union is the result of appreciation of and respect for one another, of living happily together, and of learning to love one another realistically.

Warmth, tenderness, even passion cannot be conjured up on demand; they *develop* as a result of affection, thoughtful-

172

ness, and consideration. For example, the individual who grew up afraid of sex, annoyed by it, or feeling that, somehow, it wasn't decent or nice may, at first, find difficulty in making a satisfactory sexual adjustment in marriage because his or her fear and guilt hold him back. If this person can be assured of his or her partner's sympathetic and patient understanding, immature attitudes toward sex can be outgrown. They need not block two mature people more than temporarily in finding love and deep satisfaction in a marriage relationship.

Understand the role of money. The question of what each partner considers *sufficient* financial security can cause unreasonable demands. An immature wife can "push" a husband in order to satisfy her greediness or social ambitions; she may even force a husband to give up a chosen profession because he "will not make enough money" to support her. She wants not only the best he can afford—but something better than her friends have!

On the other hand, an immature husband may demand that his wife be economically as well as psychologically dependent on him. He may so arrange the spending of money that he retains authority over all expenditures; yet he refuses to allow his wife to earn money because, he says, her doing so would reflect on his ability as a wage earner. Actually, he fears that she may become independent, possibly competing with him for control in the family or for status outside it.

A wife who is *forced* to remain at home may resent what she considers her husband's freedom—"At least, he's not tied down to cooking and cleaning and washing diapers." This feeling is particularly likely to develop if a husband fails to appreciate or if he ignores his wife's contribution to the success of their marriage and to the comfort of their home. On the other hand, a husband's work, rightly, will absorb much of his time and energy. Only an immature wife will resent his job or consider it a rival for her husband's attention.

To have or not to have children. The person who is happily married is optimistic about the present and emotionally ready to invest in the future. By wanting a child, a mature individual is reaffirming his belief that life is worth living, and that he, as a person, has something worthwhile to contribute to life and to another human being—namely, his child. For such a person child rearing is the most satisfying experience in life. Since it is unrealistic to expect a child to give a parent as much love, attention, and care as a parent has given him, the time, energy, and affection lavished on a child *is* a genuine investment in the future. Children are capable of returning some of the love they receive from their parents; *their* way of reacting to love is to grow into a happy, secure maturity.

If a marriage seems to be failing, some desperate young people may ask, will having a child bring them closer together? Neither science nor magic has produced any miracle which can transform a child-adult at his or her baby's birth into a mature adult! If the immature couple's responsibilities have irked them, if they prefer to fritter away their time, to be always "on the go," and to throw money around —if spending an evening together, making a home, and planning for the future bore them, then a child should make

174

them stay at home and like it! The child will merely be considered, unconsciously of course, as another tiresome responsibility, even though they never betray this fact in words.

If the young people's problem is that both are infants striving for advantage over one another by means of tantrums, tears, threats, and humiliations, the child will be another instrument in the struggle to dominate one another. If they must compete with one another, they will compete for the child's favor. If one of them must lean, the child will be resented as a rival for the attention of his or her spouse. In short, if the couple cannot love one another because they love only themselves, they have nothing to give a child. Marital unhappiness is one of the major causes of delinquency and emotional disturbance in children!

Learn to talk to one another. Mature young people *want* to face problems together; they want to learn gradually to understand one another better. The famous Kinsey report *Sexual Behavior in the Human Female* concludes that the most important factor in all happy marriages is the determination of both young people to make the marriage work— "the will that the marriage shall stick. Where there is this determination, then other differences between the spouses may be viewed in a perspective which emphasizes the importance of maintaining the marital union."

If a somewhat insecure partner will try sensitively to listen to the other and understand what the other is actually saying and feeling, he is less likely to misinterpret words and actions as insults or as derogatory to himself. As he learns to feel less threatened, he becomes less fearful. He

relaxes his defenses. The energy thus released can be de-
voted toward developing an increasingly sound personal relationship.

On the other hand, if one partner remains too much absorbed in his or her *own* feelings, it is impossible to sense
the other's needs and feelings. The more fearful and self-
centered a person is, the less he can become genuinely concerned about others—in fact, the less he can *really* talk with
people and understand their language. This does not mean
that he may not chatter easily. Really talking *with* people—
sensitive understanding, listening to what people say, and
sensing their feelings—is very different from chatter.

Genuine understanding of another person develops slowly,
sometimes painfully. For example, a young wife may have to
learn not to discuss important plans with her husband before
breakfast; he isn't "normal" until he has had his coffee. He
may have to learn not to expect breakfast until she has had
her warm bath. She may get to know that she should not
tease him to take her to dances; he feels clumsy on the dance
floor because of that football accident to his leg. He may
have discovered that she *will* go camping if he insists, but
she'd rather eat at home. They both learn to develop interest in and intelligent understanding of one another's work.
These are two mature people who *want* to learn to understand one another.

Love based on mutual understanding has a firm basis.
Two people who care deeply about one another will be able
to talk freely to one another. "If another person matters
as much to you as do you yourself, it is quite possible to
talk to this person as you have never talked to anyone before. The freedom which comes from this expanding of

176

one's world of satisfaction and security to include two people, linked together by love, permits exchanges of nuances of meaning and investigations without fear of rebuff or humiliation." *

The Good Marriage

Your basic idea about marriage and what it is for is of tremendous importance in determining the quality *your* marriage relationship will have. Indisputably, no marriage can rise much above the level of the personal qualities of the partners involved. A marriage relationship, in the last analysis, will be dependent on the degree of emotional maturity of each partner; on the capacity each has developed for generosity and wholehearted affection; and on the willingness of each to exert himself tirelessly in the best interests of both. It will be sustained by the integrity of both and their determination to deal honestly with each other. It will be conditioned by the skill that each has developed in knowing how to be patient as well as delightful and interesting to the other.

* Henry S. Sullivan, *Conceptions of Modern Psychiatry*, W. A. White Psychiatric Foundation, Washington, D.C., 1947, p. 20.

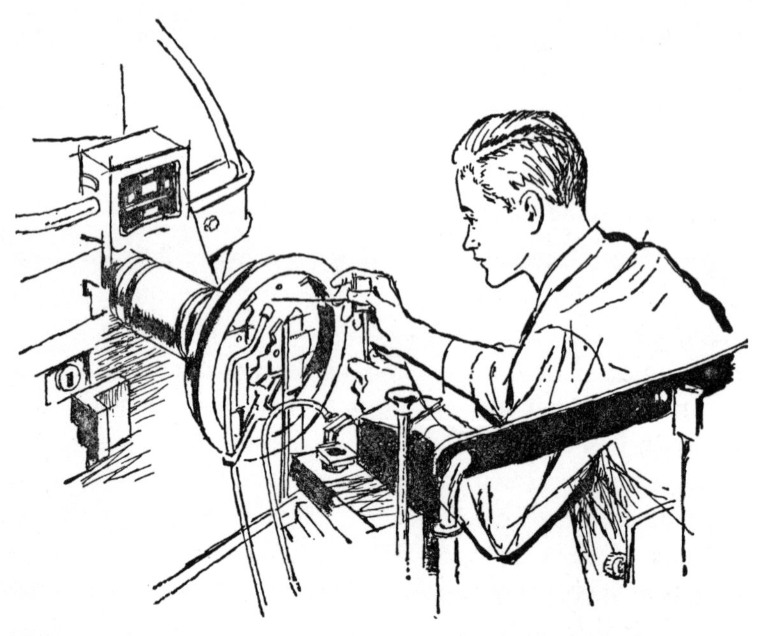

You and Your Lifework

THE PURPOSE of this chapter is not to discuss how to choose, prepare for, enter upon, and succeed in a vocation. Many books are available to help you with these problems. This chapter's aim is, rather, to help you to understand that work is a vital force in building up and maintaining your personality. Only immature people describe work as a form of punishment or oppression—whether they refer to the job by which they earn a living or some other responsibility involving effort.

178

Work as the Mature Person's Way of Life

A mature teenager looks forward eagerly to the time when he will be "on his own." To want and to hold a job means to want independence and responsibility, to seek one's security in these rather than in dependence on others. Naturally, a teenager considers the advantages of running his own affairs and anticipates the freedom which results from financial independence. However, he sees not only the money which will keep him alive and the status which will be accorded him as an adult; a mature teenager understands that work reinforces and consolidates his self-respect. A job is visible evidence that his knowledge and ability have been recognized by society.

Work presents you with daily opportunities to express yourself, to be creative, to develop new skills and talents, then to appraise your efforts objectively in relation to your coworkers. You may learn, for example, to ask yourself whether you are doing as well as you can if you limit either the quantity or character of your work by the capacity of the person next to you who may not be as competent or well-trained as you. You may begin to understand that both manual and intellectual effort are important and necessary in our economy. As you grow in skill and experience, you move, by your own efforts, into ever-wider fields of endeavor. Thus, work provides you lasting satisfaction.

Being happy in your work implies that you have not only willingly assumed the responsibilities of work as one aspect of your growth toward maturity, but also that you have carefully chosen your work in terms of your pattern for "self-development." Your satisfaction and consequent

179

achievement in a job depend upon whether that job seems to you to give you what you most desire from life. This means, again, that you must *know what you want.*

You will be "happy" in your job, well adjusted in it, and able to progress in it if it enables you to become the kind of person you envision yourself, to live the kind of life you crave in the kind of community you like, to own the kind of home you want to live in, where you can have the kind of friends you want, indulge in the pleasures you enjoy, and develop the interests, aptitudes, and values to which you wish to devote your life. Your work must *build up,* or at least contribute to the self-image you hold.

If you want, above all, to make money, to rise in social status, to exceed in personal success the level reached by your parents, to belong to the country club, to be a power in your community, you need to scrutinize each possible job in terms of "Will this get me there?" Similarly, if you are the kind of person who does his best work alone, experimenting in a laboratory or working with figures, work which gives you opportunity for solitude will be the only work congenial and appropriate for you.

A dissatisfied, unhappy individual who is in a job simply because it was the first one available or because his family or economic pressure forced him into it will never be a great success. His "heart is not in his work"—you have heard this very descriptive phrase. It says something basic—that one cannot do one's best unless one is in a situation in which one's entire "self" is involved.

On the other hand, when your "heart *is* in your work," work is not a necessary evil to be tolerated because you need money in order to buy satisfactions elsewhere. The person whose only desire is to do as little work as possible and be paid as much as possible is either immature or in the wrong job. This is equally true of the person who seems to have shifted his emphasis from pride in his work to dreams of early retirement, social benefits, or recreation!

Naturally, no human being *always* loves his job. There are times when everyone resents the alarm clock's ring, when we feel lazy and don't want to work. However, if people procrastinate too frequently about getting to work, they may actually be worrying about their inadequacy in the job; they may fear failure in its new or unfamiliar aspects. These people either have insufficient confidence in themselves or lack purpose and direction in their lives. Even you may sometimes find yourself reluctant to tackle a new job although you assure yourself that, deep down, you are certain—once you have begun—you will enjoy the challenge of the new!

Everyone possesses the power to grow into and with a task. However, before this power can operate, you must force yourself to go to work and make some small start at the day's task! Thus, you find that "getting into the swing" of work is easier than you thought. Confidence that you can perform a task creditably grows *as you work*.

However, some people actively resist work. These are generally of two types: those who are unable to face the responsibility of growing up and those who are unable to accept themselves. The first-named may *say* that they want work; they may believe that they are humiliated by their inability to find it and to earn their own way. Yet, unconsciously, they have made themselves unemployable because they cannot face responsibilities of growing up such as those involved in having their adequacy impersonally measured by practical performances, in having to yield to authority, in having to assume responsibility, in having to make decisions and to face consequences, or in having to face a daily schedule or a budget.

The second type of person feels that he does not have a worthy self. Therefore, he cannot give *himself* to a job any more than he can give himself in marriage. He cannot submit to give-and-take in an unfamiliar situation lest he lose his "self." He wants to keep what he has. For such a person, work is a painful necessity. It cannot give the worker self-respect or pride in accomplishment because he is unable to use his abilities. This person may talk gloomily of being "pushed around" or overworked, yet he will go to great lengths to avoid work or "get out of" any assigned task. He will act as though work is something to be eliminated if possible, or at least reduced. When he has a job, he works only because he would rather work than starve or be labeled lazy.

A person who feels worthless may have convinced himself that no one will employ him or keep him in their employ. By his persistent failure to find or hold a job, he may be punishing himself for being worthless. Again, he may, unconsciously, harbor so much resentment toward his parents and the world that he is "getting back" at them by forcing them to support him. This may happen with people of good mental ability and excellent training. Emotional maturity is not necessarily related to education or high mentality!

A Job "Meant for You"

A person's work should furnish him, not only a variety of human contacts, but also the status accorded one who con-
182

tributes to needs which the group considers important, who shares in common effort, and who displays social skills esteemed by the group. When a person's work is respected as valuable to other people, when he is accepted and liked by his coworkers, the mature person forgets that he may not be as educated as some, as cultured as others, as bright as someone else. He gives what he can and does not feel inferior because his contribution is not like someone else's. His energy is constantly renewed and channeled into doing an ever-better job. Thus, his life gains continuing purpose and direction.

A mature teenager approaches a job with some knowledge of what it promises in present and in future satisfactions, specific information about what it demands, and a realistic estimate of the degree to which his qualifications meet the demands. In order to judge intelligently whether a given situation may develop into the "job meant for you," a teenager must know himself well enough to recognize his special needs, particularly his emotional expectations from a job.

Without embarrassment or apology, he must, realistically, answer for himself such questions as the following: How much physical and nervous strain can you stand? How much sleep do you need? Have you any physical disabilities or history of illnesses which necessitate work in the open, or sedentary work, or work where there is a minimum of noise and confusion, or work where there is as little—or as much—change of position as possible? Do you like work which entails travel, even danger or adventure—or do you need to "settle down" in one place? Do you like many people about you because you are likely to depend upon your work as the source of your friendships? In fact, might you choose to stay on a given job primarily because you have friends there?

Perhaps you do not know yourself well enough to know what you want. True, you cannot expect yourself to be ready, at seventeen or eighteen, to make a vocational *choice* which you will "stick to" for life. Studies have shown that teenagers should be able to identify a vocational *field*, not make a vocational choice, during their high school years. Between the ages of seventeen and twenty-five, however, most young people's plans begin to stabilize if they evaluate themselves and their job experiences realistically.

Teenagers will be unrealistic if they do not know their *actual* potentialities. Perhaps they have developed an exaggerated idea of their worth—or lack of it! Some teenagers, pampered at home or overestimated at school because of athletic prowess, academic, literary, artistic, or social success, have no respect for hard work nor any conception of the value of money. Haven't you known teenagers who scorn as unworthy of their idea of "success" the beginning wage an employer offers? From their viewpoint, no prospective employer shows proper appreciation of them!

Sometimes high school, even college graduates, expect a career just to "open up"—as though the transition from school to work were no more effort than going from one classroom to another. This, too, is unrealistic. It seems not to occur to them that they must plan for years for the "right" vocational choice for *them*—while now they need actually to *hunt* for a first job in a field they consider promising. They must, therefore, be able to accept the delays and embarrassments of being an applicant—then the uncertain

184

status usually accorded a "newcomer." A mature teenager faces the fact that getting a job involves honestly wanting one, taking initiative in looking actively for one, displaying reasonable capacity in locating job opportunities and showing sufficient enthusiasm and ability to convince a prospective employer that one has pride in doing one's work speedily and well.

You need to know yourself. Is it evident from the foregoing discussion that knowing what you *really want* to do is not a simple problem to be solved by one procedure such as matching interests with occupations or taking a test of mental capacity? Any "expert" who claims that he or she can give you *all* the answers is a quack! People are complex. Many factors determine what you really want! For example, how many sound, practical reasons can you give for *your* current vocational choice?

Some teenagers *say* that they know what they want; later they decide that what they thought they wanted was a reflection of their identification with parents or an admired adult. Other teenagers are vague and changeable in their job interests; still others "have no idea." Some are concerned about their indecision; others want to be told what to do. Some take it for granted that they're "too young to know their own minds"; they take no responsibility for learning about their potentialities. Still others are eager to try out and evaluate their interests, skills, and abilities.

When teenagers have numerous interests, but little valid knowledge about themselves and less realistic information about the world of work, their occupational choices will be made in a vacuum, or they will be based on scanty facts and no experience. They may even be determined by

185

childish fantasies of glamor, adventure, or prestige. In fact, teenagers like this may never actually *choose any* job; they merely make a series of tentative "grabs" at the *nearest* job without consideration of "Where will this lead me?"

The emotionally mature teenager delays his or her *final* determination of and preparation for an occupation until he has had opportunity to think, inquire, look, listen, and explore. *Final* occupational choice is an almost irreversible decision because training for and entering upon an occupation produces—in fact, demands—changes in you as a person, as well as an investment in time and money. Therefore, it is very important that your choice be based on a realistic estimate of the entire situation which is "you."

Self-knowledge can be *facilitated* through testing and counseling. A mature teenager will seek professional help in learning to know himself. Counselors are found, these days, in many industries, high schools, colleges, government employment offices, and community agencies. Reputable vocational counselors are not prophets or magicians; they would not—if they could—tell you exactly what to do and what not to do. However, they can help teenagers to think in terms of "What am I now?" and "What may I become if I work at it?" Most young people *want direction* in the process of making up their minds about future study and work. *Valid* information about themselves is the soundest basis for wise consideration of possible alternatives.

Counselors can help a teenager, through tests, interviews, and observation to determine his aptitudes, interests, and potentialities and to appraise personality growth. For example, a counselor in an industry or school may solicit appraisals of a given teenager from teachers or foremen,
  186

coaches or club leaders, office help, janitors, fellow-students
or coworkers who have seen the teenager working, playing,
loafing—seeking, meeting, or shirking responsibility—enjoying or evading class and social activities—dealing adequately with difficult situations, or meeting them in an immature fashion. On the basis of factual evidence like this,
the counselor is able to recommend ways in which a teenager may become a more adequate person or employee.
From these appraisals and from a battery of tests—of ability,
achievement, range of aptitudes, interests, and emotional
stability—a teenager and a counselor can discuss the teenager's vocational alternatives—and his future—realistically.

Known potentialities and weaknesses constitute the point
of reference from which they plan together how to "work
things out." As a result, a teenager may decide intelligently
upon further training in specific skills and accomplishments,
or may find that he needs to aim primarily at increasing
ability to work with people or more ease and confidence in
social relationships. It may be that specialized training in
one skill or remedial work in some school subject is suggested to him. Possibly, he finds that he needs to develop
sounder work habits. He may even decide to postpone
formal training in some area until he has had a tryout work
experience and has discovered whether he actually "belongs"
in this type of work.

Sources of training are generally suggested by counselors;
these are evaluated in terms of a teenager's specific needs.
If formal education in a college is too expensive, for example,
a counselor may suggest to one teenager that he take the
training sponsored by the business, industry, bank, or union
in which he works, or by the local adult school or community

college. Again, a teenager may find that opportunities to learn skills and gain valuable experience are available through informal club programs, volunteer work in community agencies, part-time positions or tryout work experience programs sponsored by his school or college.

You need to try yourself out. The seriousness with which a teenager gathers factual information about himself and about the vocational field in which he is interested and the degree to which he spends his time and effort trying himself out in activities allied to his chosen field all indicate the *reality* of his expressed interest. Has a would-be reporter worked on a school, campus, or trade paper? Does he or she know what it means to keep the seat of the pants on the seat of the chair, write and rewrite in order to meet a deadline, even if he misses a football game or his dinner? Has he rewritten and read proof until his fingers ached from banging the typewriter and his eyes stung? Has he learned to make contacts with people and "get the story," no matter how much time or persistence it takes? Does he like to listen to people—so that he gets his facts straight? Does he read newspapers regularly? Is he making the most of his education as preparation for his future work? If someone "interested" in journalism answers negatively, it would be wise for him to find out what reporting is *really* like and what type of preparation, personal characteristics, and temperament it requires!

When teenagers have fair assurance, based on valid information about themselves, that their vocational interests are genuine and realistic, they would be wise to plan to evaluate themselves and their potentialities in real situations.

188

For example, each teenager who thinks he wants to spend his life doing a certain type of work needs to explore the day-by-day routine of the job. Then he can honestly appraise himself with, "Can you take it? Do you really want to?" Practically no teenager knows, before his or her first day on a job, what it is really like to work from nine to five, to be on time every day, to stick to a scheduled lunch hour, to remain at a desk, at a machine, or at a counter ready to serve customers for nearly eight hours at a stretch.

Perhaps you find that, in terms of the kind of person you really are, dreams of childhood just do not make sense. For example, one teenager's beautiful picture of himself or herself as a doctor followed by eager students who hang on his words as he makes rounds in a hospital—or the vision of a crisp, unstained nurse's uniform—may fade abruptly after he or she enters a hospital as a volunteer aide. The smells of blood, bedpans, and disinfectants alone "get him down"—to say nothing of taking responsibility for people's lives!

Realistic occupational decisions are based on facts, not words about yourself. Experience alone can assure you that an "interest" is genuine, a job feels "right," the emotional and social values it represents are ones you can accept, its disadvantages are ones with which you can live, the qualities it demands are ones you actually possess.

A tryout experience may save time, money, and effort. Unhappiness, even failure, in one's work can result from following an unrealistic goal. True, it takes an experience of failure to convince some people that a certain goal *is* unrealistic for them. However, even then, people can profit by this experience if they evaluate the failure as necessary exploration made to free themselves from an illusion. Now, they can turn their released "self," wholeheartedly, toward another objective.

On the basis of *some* known facts about yourself, you make an *initial* decision about a field of work. Suppose you decide to secure advanced education to prepare yourself for a *more distant* goal. Sometimes, you find that it is necessary to hold a job in an unrelated field in order to buy time and money to finance the studies. This may be disheartening; but you're not "off the track" if you keep your eyes on your objective—your *final* occupational choice.

"Finding" *the* job for you is a developmental process which takes place over a period of years—a process of understanding and implementing your "self." Before you finally reach this goal, you will, undoubtedly, have learned to compromise between the "self" you thought you were and the "self" you discover you really are, between what you thought you wanted and what you find you really want, between what you must do now—because of financial pressures —and what you can work toward if you use your money for future training or education. You will have learned to handle the choice between what you want to do and what you feel you must do to secure the approval of people important to you.

The Human Relations You Create

Research studies about vocations have shown that each person *can* be successful in a number of occupations. *Whether* he is successful depends much less on his technical skill than on his attitude toward a job and on his possession of certain personal characteristics and human qualities.

When a study of General Motors industries in South Chicago was made, for example, it was discovered that, over a three-year period, 91 per cent of the employees discharged had failed in some aspect of human relationships—particularly had they failed to understand the rights and feelings of others.

Often, a person's disappointment, frustration, and even feeling of monotony about a job—even about a school—may be due to failure to get along with his coworkers—or his classmates. Ability to get along with people, the reader knows, depends on a person's sound attitude toward himself. If a person can acknowledge what is right and good about himself, he finds it easier to accept and live with the things that are wrong about himself—and others. If he is objective with himself—and with others—he realizes that assets always outweigh liabilities in a really useful person.

Basic to anyone's happiness on his job and ability to do his best work is the ability to develop in himself and in his coworkers positive attitudes toward their mutual concerns. Suppose that you were in charge of assisting employees new on the job. If you have been a big brother or sister to a new student in your school, you understand this responsibility.

How will you make people feel comfortable about their work—and themselves—and you? You will need, not only genuinely to enjoy people, to know how to talk with them and how to develop a satisfactory give-and-take relationship, you will need also to sense people's difficulties, know "how things look" to someone new and strange, know when and how to help in such a way that your help does not seem to be given patronizingly, grudgingly, or even resentfully.

Some people give assistance or directions in a way that exasperate those they think they are helping. Yet, they may fervently long for skill and ease in human relationships! Some person who looks and sounds like "the big I" may not mean to brag. He may *really know* how to do something; he just hasn't learned to explain it. He may talk too much and help too little. "The sourpuss" may truly *want* to help other people; but may be afraid to offer friendship and help for fear people will not like him or will scorn his assistance. The "apple-polisher" may actually be so unsure of himself in social relationships that he thinks fawning on people is necessary to gain their cooperation.

Can you become someone who has confidence in other people and in their desire to do the "right" thing? What do your brothers and sisters, friends and classmates say? If you can accept your own awkwardness, stupidity, and fear, you can help other people when they need to face "what is wrong." If you have failed successfully, you are humble but not timid. With such an attitude, you can help others pick themselves up after a stumble and go on courageously. On the other hand, if you have succeeded gracefully, you are not arrogant; you can assist others to "grow without swelling." No matter what problem anyone faces with someone else, it will pass; but the human relations one has created will remain. People will not easily forget the way you made them *feel* about you and about themselves!

Your attitude toward authority. If you are not in a job now, the quality of your relationships inside your family is the most important indication of your attitude toward authority. Several recent vocational studies have proved that the relationship of an employee with an employer reflects

192

the employee's relationship with his or her father. The father in every family represents the outside world.

Each teenager is likely to carry over into his or her job the pattern of responding to authority which he learned at home. You take *yourself* to work. You cannot wake up different from what you were yesterday because you are beginning that "big new job" today any more than because you are being married today.

Some teenagers who rebel against their parents' authority do not understand that, sometimes, authority supports and protects them; sometimes, it thwarts them for the good of the group. A few teenagers boast that *no* authority will control them. Often these, so-called, willful and obstreperous young people are not "unspanked." On the other hand, they may be overpunished. Parents may have been so strict with them, have held the controls so tightly, that the teenagers never developed their own controls.

To such teenagers, an employer is not a person; he is a symbol of authority. Perhaps he must be placated, possibly taken advantage of, cajoled, or despised secretly. When some teenagers talk to "the Boss," they agree with all he says; they do what they are told without question. Others argue or wheedle to get what they want—even belittle themselves or resort to self-pity.

One teenager with deep fear of authority may seem uninterested in his work or uncooperative when, actually, he or she is eager to please but "scared to death" whenever "the Boss" is around observing his work. This teenager may have learned at home that he or she would not be given consideration or approval unless he erased himself and became a doormat. Another teenager who seems "smart-alecky" and "know-it-all" to his "Boss" may, in reality, be eager to please and be working hard to learn *some* of the answers. In trying to prove to his Boss that he knows *all* the answers, he may be overacting because he found that, in order to gain attention or approval at home, or to get something he wanted or needed, he had to yell, argue, boast, demand, threaten, or throw tantrums.

No one is employed very long before his employer knows his characteristic response to authority; whether he is quiet, "obedient," afraid of his own ideas, rebelling loudly against "restrictions" and suggestions or able to ask for and accept directions, help, and criticism as necessary. Because most people cannot work alone any more than they can live apart from people, most teenagers will, at some time, be dependent on the authority inherent in employers and colleagues. Seldom in life can one escape authority.

Some teenagers have mixed feelings about authority. They need "someone who will take the responsibility," but are suspicious lest the authority take advantage of them, exploit them or "let them down." They do not trust others because they do not trust themselves. Such individuals distrust coworkers as well as the "authority." They cannot consider the contribution of another as valuable; they see it only as competition. They become hostile if the "authority" praises or rewards a colleague. Even a compliment to someone else is interpreted as an intentional slight to them! Although they know that the recognition is just, they are envious.

So fearful may these individuals become that they see insults and threats in innocent remarks and actions; they may interpret suggestions as reflections on their competence.
194

Consequently, to "protect" themselves or to build themselves up, they may try to undermine their colleagues to the employer; then they may attack the employer with their colleagues! Such people are chronically looking for "a catch" in everything, a weakness in everyone.

Some individuals have so low an opinion of themselves that they continually fawn on others and flatter them. Such people may be considered, by the undiscerning, as charming people because they build up another's ego even as they disparage themselves. Contempt of self, however, is evidence of lack of genuine respect for or confidence in others. You judge others *as* you judge yourself, you know!

The person with immature attitudes toward authority is not an effective worker. His fear of people blocks his efficiency; his energy goes into worrying about what they think of him and his work. Often he is unable to talk easily to people. Actually, he is afraid of them. Nevertheless, when he keeps up his defenses against them, they, in turn, misunderstand his silence, shun him as "highhat," or ridicule him as "a dope." He becomes more anxious and hostile as he finds himself "left out."

His insecurity and unhappiness may result in his becoming careless of valuable equipment, becoming accident-prone, shutting himself up inside himself, spreading rumors, writing on toilet walls, inciting others to rebellion against the unfairness of "authority," or changing jobs frequently. "This job is not for me" may actually be such a person's way of protecting himself from anxiety. He blames the job, not himself, for "the state he is in"!

Mature use of authority. When you yourself have a position of authority, how do you look to your fellow students?

While you function as committee chairman, class officer, student council representative, fraternity president, team manager, editor of the school paper—or any other position of prestige which you hold in school or on campus—how do your classmates think you handle authority? Are you a catalytic agent or a switchboard? Do you release other people to be their best because you believe in them, or must you force everything to "go through you" so that you can "check up" on people or gain credit for their accomplishments?

The mature person willingly accepts the responsibility accompanying authority; but he refrains from using force. He knows that, although he is the *designated* authority, real power lies with his coworkers—whether he or she is club president, supervisor of a road gang, head nurse, sales manager, or chairman of a corporation. *This* power he nurtures and develops; he can even accept a decision not his own if the group has found one better!

Sharing authority is not a threat to a person with this conception of authority: you, as club officer, assume that *both* you and your classmates have knowledge and skill. Sharing these, you work together to solve mutual problems. Both feel reassuring support from the other, yet each is free to *do* his best and *be* his best. You know that everyone wants to be responsible, as far as possible, for himself and his assigned tasks, yet, in many areas, everyone wants leadership and direction.

An individual with this conception of authority refrains from personal favors or criticisms; he helps people to gain their rewards from work they do together, to understand and learn from their mistakes and wrong decisions—as he

196

himself tries to do! Suppose that, in a rushed moment, he
made an arbitrary rule to which his coworkers or classmates,
rightly, immediately reacted with open resentment of his
"dictatorship."

Intellectually, he knows that if a new rule or policy is
likely to cause an "explosion," it is best to discuss it logically
and impersonally with everyone concerned, not "to spring"
it on people. Surprised, people are often taken off their
guard, and speak hastily and emotionally. Then their pride
forbids them to retreat from the position assumed. If people are "stirred up," they cannot think clearly; reason plays
a secondary role to emotion.

Since this person's momentary lack of foresight created a
"blowup," he does not force the issue. He allows everyone
to cool off. Then he may try logical persuasion. Should
it prove "too little and too late," this mature individual probably compromises gracefully. Not everyone can successfully
control his emotional reactions; but he who *can* keep his
head, admit his mistake, and learn from a wrong decision
has a great advantage over those who cannot think clearly.
A mature person might even be able to use this incident to
help others to understand *their behavior* and *the issues* involved—as well as the "blowup"!

Emotional "blowups" are inevitable in human relationships; but they vary in intensity from person to person. We
all "blow up" sometimes. In general, being rested, feeling
peppy and happy make a person's self-control relatively easy.
Too much fatigue, boredom or frustration, too few permanent satisfactions, a low opinion of oneself and consequent
lack of adjustment account for *chronic* "blowups."

The mature person acts on the assumption that there are

better ways than force. He is deeply certain that people can be *trusted* to do their best; they need not be bribed or driven. He understands that most people *want* to use their energy and brains to develop standards of performance and efficiency adequate to their responsibilities.

The Woman Who Works

Could any teen-age girl have read this chapter halfheartedly, thinking to herself, "A job is only temporary for me—until I marry"? Frances Perkins, former Secretary of Labor, said in a Job Seminar sponsored by *Glamour Magazine* in 1953 that more married women work than ever before. In 1952, at the time of the last census, nearly one-fourth of the couples who had set up their own households after marriage were both working. Moreover, the trend is that women who leave the world of work for marriage return to it some years later.

Homemakers are coming to be looked upon as women who enter and leave the labor market at various periods in their lives. "Now and for the foreseeable future it will be necessary for women to equip themselves to work outside the home as well as in it. To this end part-time and volunteer jobs are good investments for students and housewives. For today, careers rank with homemaking as a basic activity for women. Tomorrow, perhaps, the girl who's never had a job may be as rare as the man who never worked for a living." [*]

That public opinion, also, is moving in this direction is indicated by an author who thus discusses woman's contribution to society: "I have never been able to believe that a

[*] *Glamour Magazine*, September, 1953, p. 217.

198

woman's task in life is limited to her children.—There is an urge to creativeness which lies underneath and deeper above and beyond the begetting of children.—Women have a contract with life itself, which is not discharged by the mere procreation of their species. Men recognize and try to honor this contract in themselves as a matter of course. Their contribution to life vibrates with their passionate rebellion against the narrowly conceived idea that would restrict their role to that of protectors and feeders of women and children. They do not acknowledge and respect the same thing so readily in women. Perhaps until they do the world will not see the full creative relationship that life intends there should be between men and women." *

The Job Seminar of *Glamour Magazine* emphasized, further, that most young women who go into business begin in one of nine vital jobs: messenger or mail girl, receptionist, clerk, typist, office machine operator, stenographer, secretary, telephone operator, or salesgirl. Perhaps this is not a teenager's picture of the "ideal job." If you began in one of these positions, what would you see in your job?

Girls contributing to the Job Seminar said that the six most satisfying elements of their work were: the chance to help others, the opportunity to learn, the worthwhile accomplishment, the contact with people, the challenge presented, and the variety of duties demanded. True, not every messenger or typist displays initiative, resourcefulness, or adaptability, but those girls who do bring plus qualities to these jobs. They are noticed and become candidates for more responsible jobs. They are the farseeing individuals who,

* Laurens Van der Post, *Venture to the Interior,* William Morrow & Company, Inc., New York, 1951, p. 25.

while recognizing the importance of salary and other considerations, still regard these as less permanent sources of contentment in a job than the six values listed above. These are the mature people who know that a job is more than just a way to make a living; it is also a way to live fully, wisely, and well.

You and Your Schooling

For many teenagers, your present full-time job is becoming educated. Are you getting the most out of your schooling —in terms of subject matter you can learn, abilities you can discover and try out, habits of achievement you can develop, and attitudes toward people you can demonstrate? Are you actively seeking to learn all you can of the best that has been thought and done on many important subjects, not in order to accumulate this learning in dead storage but to stockpile resources which can be mobilized in your contribution to life and your life's work? Suppose you examine each of these areas:

What Are You "Taking"?

Do you look upon your school or college experience as a series of disconnected, somewhat boring episodes called classes? Or do you envision education as a program planned to help a maturing individual to understand himself, discover and explore his potentialities, and acquire ideas and attitudes which will help him to live with some security and feeling of belonging in a complicated world? Look at a few of your subjects.

What is your attitude toward science? Do you want to become informed and literate in science in order to cope somewhat more intelligently with a scientific age in which you need not only to understand what makes gadgets run, but also how to use gadgets without deadening your own personality or interfering with other people's rights—even their lives? Do you desire to become more nearly qualified to help make decisions—as you must in our democracy—about the uses of some scientific discoveries? You may, in your community, be voting for educational television or feeling the effects of the use of atomic energy in local industry. If you, yourself, are aiming for a scientific career, are you, in science classes, learning about the effect of scientific discoveries so that you may be a responsible citizen as well as a responsible scientist?

Are you learning, through your political science courses, to be concerned about good government? Are you actually participating in school and in community government? Every good school and college in the country offers you opportunities to do the first, and an increasing number of schools are setting up definite projects on which students and local government officials cooperate.

Are you, in your history class, learning to take warm interest in the backgrounds, problems, and aspirations of people in other lands? Confidence in a future in which people can live together peacefully rests on confidence in a generation of young people who will know and appreciate the background, culture, economic problems, and thinking of people all over the world, who will listen to them sympathetically and assist them to help themselves.

Are you, through your English and literature classes, learning not only to express yourself clearly so that you mean what you say, but to say it confidently so that your tone of voice, facial expression, and choice of words convey to others an impression of balance, maturity, thoughtfulness, and consideration of others?

Are you using the content of your literature course to become acquainted with situations and people who, throughout the ages, have faced problems similar to those you now face as you struggle to develop standards, values, or beliefs? In other words, are you becoming a capable and cultivated human being whose intellectual and spiritual powers are continually growing? The philosopher John Stuart Mill said that "men are men" before they are manufacturers or factory workers or physicians. If they make themselves capable and ethical men—and women—they will make themselves capable and ethical workers.

Moreover, in preparation for many of today's careers, sensitivity to the problems of human beings is a major consideration. While you may have learned that, at present, there is an urgent demand for engineers, are you aware also that the most urgent *requirement* is for engineers who can cope with human problems? Industrial executives, in increasing numbers, are saying that only engineers so trained can save our technology from becoming a heartless and eventually a helpless monster. Do you know that doctors are demanding that preparation for medicine now include intensive study of behavior along with training in natural sciences? Emphasis in practicing medicine is shifting from exclusive consideration of the patient's illness to the patient as a human being.

Do you now, as future homemaker and parent, take advantage of opportunities in schools, colleges, and communities to learn about home management and family living? Many schools and colleges have courses or regularly scheduled group discussions in modern living, psychology, child development, insurance and budgeting, marriage and family living; there are chefs' clubs, home repair clubs, interior decorating or home safety clubs, and hobby groups of all kinds. If your school or college does not offer you this assistance, interest your friends, your parents, and your neighbors in presenting a specific request to school authorities. Schools and colleges are eager to meet the needs of communities; therefore, communities always have the kind of education they want—or deserve!

How Do You Learn?

A well-known author in the field of child development "ventured the hypothesis that human beings from an early age have more capacity for learning to face, understand, and deal constructively with the realities of their lives than we have assumed in our psychological theories or in our educa-

204

tional practices." * Teenagers have too frequently been talked *at* and talked *down to* instead of talked *with*, then given responsibility for making their own decisions and abiding by consequences. Just as the premise of this book is that teenagers *can* learn to understand and, if necessary, change themselves, so the assumption in this chapter is that teenagers *can* educate themselves—either in school or college or through other media.

Why some people fail to learn. No teacher can *force* students to learn any more than an employer can *force* people to work. A teacher cannot fight for someone's attention or for control of a class and, at the same time, help individuals to learn. Learning implies guidance, insight, and understanding of problems in human relations.

A war of nerves with the teacher does nothing to advance a teenager's education. It hinders it; it is evidence of problems which "keep your mind off your work." Since he carries himself to school just as he carries himself into a job or into marriage, all of a teenager's difficulties go with him.

You're not the only one with problems! Here is Bill. Bill is worried because his parents do not like him and are always comparing him to a "brilliant" brother. He thinks they are disappointed in him: Bill is always getting himself into scrapes. Carol is lonely. She wants friends more than she wants anything else in the world. Joan is worried about her sick mother; she is also deeply hurt because her father did not trust her enough to tell her, until the night before they left the city where they had lived for years, that the

* Arthur T. Jersild, *In Search of Self*, Bureau of Publications, Teachers College, Columbia University, New York, 1952, p. 3.

family was moving to a new community. Then she "got off
on the wrong foot" with her family and the school authorities in the new school because she got in the wrong gang
and because the school attendance officer thought she was
playing truant.

A great many students have serious problems—teachers
find numerous young people "who have had a long history
of being pushed about, neglected, or rejected, with damag-
ing effects on their attitudes toward themselves—a great
many young people whose lack of assurance concerning
themselves makes them uncomfortable in their relations with
others. Therefore, countless young people are using and
enjoying only a small portion of their resources and are
living meager lives." *

No wonder they can't make themselves want to study!
Troubled people find that they cannot concentrate or remember. They may also experience fears. They may resort to pranks, crudeness, and impudence without knowing
why. They may become activity "hounds" and try to "get
into everything" in order to become "known." Or they
may become excessively guarded or perfectionistic; they
may tend to do nothing or say nothing until they are certain that they are "right." Possibly they want to sleep all
the time. Actually, they do these things because they feel
overwhelmed by adjustments they must make. They feel
panicky because they have made some ineffective attempts
at solutions and found themselves more unpopular than ever
at home, at school, on campus, or in the neighborhood.

Should you have similar problems—instead of trying to
force yourself to learn—turn your energy to removing *ob-*

* Arthur T Jersild, *In Search of Self*, Bureau of Publications, Teachers College, Columbia University, New York, 1952, p. 6.

stacles which *prevent you* from learning. What you need is information and direction in freeing yourself from the battle inside yourself. You need to understand behavior. If you look at the meaning of your acts, not at the acts themselves, you will learn—not that you are "bad" because you act like that—but that you act like that because you are troubled. If you gain this understanding, you may realize that the adults who hurt you probably are also troubled.

When they are troubled or upset, they also do what may look to others like "the wrong thing." For instance, the attendance officer who, without checking his facts, accused Joan of truancy may have had a fight with his wife that morning, may have had a sick headache, or may have just suffered through a series of conferences full of criticism and complaint against the school. Joan's father and Bill's parents may honestly have believed that they were doing the right thing. Joan's father, knowing how difficult it would be for her to leave her city friends, may not have told her about the projected move because he wanted to "let her be happy as long as possible." Bill's parents may feel that their comparison of Bill to his brother may spur Bill on to accomplishments of his own.

You want to learn. When you are freed of obstacles inside yourself, you find that learning is a normal process. Every healthy, well-adjusted human being has a *drive* continually *to learn* more. You want to grow in the direction of expressing your "self" more adequately and achieving more nearly the extent of your potentialities.

Your school can only facilitate your learning. It is merely an adjunct to what is within the person who is growing. *Your* education begins with a careful analysis of what kind of person you are and what level of maturity you have attained; it implies your awareness of where you are going. Your *actual* growth, however, is a process over which no school or college—not even your home—has final control. Learning comes from within. Education *can assist* you toward self-confidence and self-fulfillment. But it *cannot mold* you; you will grow in the direction *you choose* to grow. No one can educate you in spite of yourself. Your school offers you resources. Your acceptance of these—your learning from what is offered—depends upon whether you put forth the effort to learn. No one can do this for you.

Education, literally, means to lead out, not to pound in. Skillful teachers will try to help teenagers to unleash their normal, constructive energy and to become efficient learners. This is no simple task. It takes discernment to set up situations which encourage teenagers to help themselves. Does it seem, comparatively, easier to demand that teenagers perform definite tasks or suffer the consequences? If teachers attempt to *force* teenagers to do as they are told, many teenagers will expend time and energy trying to *avoid* the command. Besides what they will really *learn* from such an experience is resentment against teachers!

The laws of learning. How do you envision the role of the learner and the role of the teacher? If you are to learn, you must be able to *trust* your ability to learn and other people's desire to teach you—again, the give-and-take of living! Can you *take* with confidence or are you afraid new knowledge may change "you"? Can you *give* what you know to others or do you hold back for fear you may have a wrong answer?

Learning, like life everywhere, comprises anxiety and confidence, joy and disappointment, success and failure,

pride and humiliation. As you struggle to master new facts
or a new skill or to free yourself from habits and attitudes
which hamper you, each step in learning may be preceded
and accompanied by anxiety, lack of self-confidence, or fear
of failure. We're all afraid we'll show how "dumb" we are
or what fools we've been! However, if you continue to
try, if you practice new skills, habits, and attitudes, gradually you learn to master each situation. From every success
comes a growing feeling of adequacy.

Studies of how learning takes place show that mastery of
a skill is preceded by readiness or desire to learn the new
skill and is accompanied by effort and practice in a variety
of situations. Changes in habits and attitudes are made
most effectively, according to studies, when one wants to
change, learns how to change, and applies what one has
learned in *many* areas of day-by-day experience. By fulfilling these conditions, you, too, can gradually gain increased
ability in expressing yourself according to your individual
talents, increased satisfaction in the knowledge that you have
overcome past fears and anxieties, increased sensitivity and
skill in developing satisfactory relationships with people.

Pleasure and deep satisfaction accompany all learning,
as the following comments of teenagers illustrate: "It's fun
to go home and show my little brother how to use a lathe."
"I like to read good books just to feel I have them inside
me." "I like the feeling, as I pass the City Hall, of knowing
how our town government is run." "I like to have my dad
feel I know something when I discuss politics with him."

Discipline. Readiness to learn, plus effort and practice,
yield mastery of a skill and change in behavior. In this process, discipline has been involved. But it has been inter-

nally, not externally applied; it has been "self"-discipline. You deliberately chose to deny yourself something, or you tried something, or you refrained from doing something because of a goal you had in mind—something you wanted enough to be willing to pay a price to secure. Discipline was something you accepted, not something imposed on you. In fact, no person and no rules can *impose* discipline on you; they can only impose penalties or administer punishment. Once you catch this idea, you are on the road to being a learner!

Many teenagers, however, confuse discipline with negative attitudes toward authority. For example, if teenagers have had problems in school, they may say that the school authorities have *disciplined* them.

It is possible to confuse discipline with habits of work. Haven't you heard teenagers excuse their failure by saying, "That teacher—or my parents—didn't *make* me work?" No one, except yourself, can *make* you work. And you *will make* yourself develop adequate work habits only if you have a goal which makes work important to you—important enough to make you *choose to work* toward that goal even on the night you miss the baseball game because you chose to study for tomorrow's science test!

Mature teenagers understand the importance of setting goals for themselves. Some high school seniors remarked ruefully, "I found I could slide through and I did." "I think people should learn to set their goals higher."—"I made poor grades my first year because I was ill—then I tried to believe that was the best I could do."—"We don't have enough pride in our work—and schools don't expect enough of us." It is, indeed, generally agreed among educators that schools

210

and colleges do not expect enough of the very intelligent students; but it is equally evident, from the remarks above, that many young people do not expect enough of themselves.

In fact, in some schools the slower students are the ones who are doing their best—who are working even beyond their capacity—and gaining small recognition for their effort; they may even be labeled failures. No one has failed in any area of life—on the job, in school, at home, in skills, or in personal relationships—if he has gained from an experience all that he is capable of absorbing. A person has truly failed when, through laziness, poor work habits, or immature attitudes, he has failed to gain from an experience what *he* might have gained. Even though he remembered certain assorted facts long enough to "squeeze through" a course, he has used his potentialities poorly.

What Are You Learning?

Your curriculum is your total experience in school or college. As you estimate how well you are taking advantage of educational opportunities, you cannot separate classes, extracurricular activities, social life, or personal relationships. Is your curriculum preparing you to contribute intelligently to family living—perhaps as a son or daughter today, but as husband or wife tomorrow? Are you learning to build satisfying human relationships, to meet vocational responsibilities, to build habits which will protect your life and health, to use the tools of communication effectively, to develop economic competence, to practice responsible citizenship, not only as voter and taxpayer, but as a participating member of your community, country, and world? Are you evolving mature spiritual and aesthetic values?

What do all these fine words mean? Simply that this country—and the world—will desperately need wise people and capable citizens willing and qualified to assume *their* share of responsibility for democracy's success. And where can they come from except the schoolroom? If our country is to continue to be a democracy, we must continue to have a people who run their own affairs. All the people, not just a few, must know what is going on and must be willing and able to make intelligent choices concerning important questions.

If you are to believe in democracy, you must learn in school to have faith in the dignity of your own human nature and in the inherent potentialities for good in every human being. You must become a mature, responsible, adjusted person able to deal with changes inevitable in our world. Are you capable of the type of reasoning, for example, which has recently created, in our country, a public opinion which grasps the basic importance to this age of sharing our resources with people everywhere?

As a citizen in a democracy, *are* you learning that everyone is valuable? Do you accept human beings, regardless of physical, racial, social, nationality, economic, or religious background and appreciate them for whatever they contribute to the common welfare? Do you believe that everyone must have opportunities and responsibilities according to his capacity? Do you evidence these beliefs in the contacts you make and the friends you choose in school, in the community, or on campus?

What effort are you making to become acquainted with students of different races and nationalities? What do you know about religions different from yours? Have you any idea what that fellow crippled with polio intends to do with his life? Not long ago, in an American high school, a boy without legs was voted most popular boy in school. What kind of person do you suppose he was? Would you have liked to know him? You miss a great thrill in school, if through fear, ignorance, or prejudice, you stick to the old Elm Street or church crowd or to the fraternity or sorority group!

Education can be a process through which people learn to think, feel, and act differently. It can help you to master your own feelings, to guide your conduct, to use your intelligence, and to grow to know yourself. Your schooling can assist you to develop and equip yourself to make your own life truly happy and "good."

It can also provide you opportunities to contribute to the welfare of others and to take part effectively in community living. Along with your *training* in responsible citizenship, have you *participated* willingly in school activities so that you feel experienced enough to take part in community activities? Of what leadership opportunities have you taken advantage in school or on campus? Are you on any student association, homeroom, club, class, or student-faculty committees? Are you on a school team? Are you a Student Government representative? Are you a library assistant, a reporter on the school or campus paper, a band or orchestra member, an assistant in the art, chemistry, shop, agriculture —or any other—department?

What elective offices have you held? When you run for office, what do you hope to accomplish—the satisfaction of beating someone else, the chance to push ahead of someone, the satisfaction of being "a big wheel"? Or do you want training in becoming a responsible leader? In this age in which everyone needs desperately to learn to understand other people's viewpoints, you have an obligation to educate yourself in the give-and-take of the conference table, the sharing of ideas, and the final fusion of many ideas into a plan of action which everyone can support. By experience in this kind of problem-solving, you develop a sense of responsibility to the people with whom you work as well as genuine understanding of what participation really means.

How much thought are you giving, in these crowded school days, to the fact that, in American industry, the work week has shrunk to forty hours and is still shrinking? What will life be like for you, in a year or two, if you are one of those workers with a thirty- or forty-hour week? You will have time on your hands. This fact is a necessary condition for the cultivation of your *own* individuality. On the other hand, time to cultivate your individuality does not guarantee that you will have individuality to cultivate unless you begin now to make the most of educational opportunities within your reach and to seek constantly for new ones.

The problem of leisure is the *problem* of how we can enrich the quality of our daily experience in *all* areas of our lives so that there will be no *problem* of leisure. Too many teenagers never see the difference between genuine leisure and just "time on their hands." They have grown up in a leisure pattern of noise and distraction hurled at them while they sat passively and were or were not amused. They have never learned about the world of self-cultivation. It is available to *you*—if you are willing to invest the time and effort involved!

214

You and Your Ideals

LIFE WILL not go on forever. Sometime there will be no
"today." This fact jars you into taking the present seriously.
Now is what matters. The past and the future exist in the
present only as they influence and change you in the present.

The way you face today and what you choose to do tomorrow determine the "self" you will be five and ten years from
now. The results of today's decisions and actions are not
limited to today; in fact, they often do not show up today.
Yet, your future is born out of your present.

Do you see each today as a continual opening out into
new possibilities on which to build your unique character as
a person? Do you understand and control the fears, angers,
overdependence, and problems of the past, the dreams and
ambitions of the future, so that what you have learned from

215

each helps direct your present decisions and actions? Or are you afraid of the present?

Do you separate yourself from reality by escaping to the "when" of the future or the "then" of the past, saying perhaps that "today" was empty; you were bored? Are you one of those people who cannot face a day free from school, errands, telephone calls, and dates—who has a good time only when time passes without your noticing it? If you so live that nothing matters to you, you *will* be bored. Boredom, however, is inner emptiness; it signifies that you have no purposes which give direction to your life. "The great long-time menace to human life is not atom bombs, but boredom." *

How You "Get" Your Values

Most teenagers *want to know* what they're living for; they keep looking for a sense of direction. They are occupied with the need for some faith. They discuss all sorts of ideas. They believe them for the moment. Afterward, they may feel that they were nonsense; they may be inclined to blush about ever having believed them.

When you are unsure of yourself and uncertain about the future, you look for answers. You need something to hold on to. We all need to live by something. President Neilson, formerly of Smith College, used to say, "It's a good thing to have an open mind—but not so open that your brains fall out."

You want, at the core of your being, a nucleus of beliefs which cannot be chipped away or blown to bits or dissolved

* Arthur E. Morgan, *Search for Purpose*, Antioch Press, Yellow Springs, Ohio, 1955, p. 165.

216

in thin air. These draw together your powers and give them focus. Until you know what you really want out of life you won't understand why, day by day, you behave as you do. What happens will seem like a series of disconnected fragments. However, you cannot "find" values. Nor will you "get" them by group discussion; you cannot take over other people's values. *Your* goals will develop as you learn *your* answer to the question, "What do *I* really want out of life?"

What some people have wanted and have found deeply satisfying has been suggested in previous chapters: know, accept, and believe in yourself; resolve your fears; guard your health; enjoy your friends; make the most of your family experience; learn to love; learn to work and to capitalize on your leisure. How did people learn these answers? From life itself! "Life is always with us if we are but willing to accept what is set before us— To the all-important question, 'What is the Way of Life?', the answer is 'Walk on'!" *

Life makes demands on everyone. When they are challenged, most teenagers find unsuspected strength in themselves. As they reply to life's challenges day by day, their values evolve from their experience. External actions are an expression of inner motives. By testing out values in your daily decisions, you learn to judge results, to believe in what you are doing, or to act more effectively next time.

In the process of living, you develop the unique values for which *you* will stand up and be counted.—"You have to find the road for yourself. No one can show it to you.— You're a man—not a mule to be led.—You may take the

* E. Graham Howe and L. Le Mesurier, *The Open Way*, Methuen & Co., Ltd., London, 1939.

wrong road; you may retreat for a while; you may even feel that you have nothing left to fall back on. But you do— you'll never slip back permanently. You may mark time for a few years. But somebody, something, turns up to give you a push in the right direction. It may be hardship and sorrow; it may be adversity. You must be ready for that. Or it may be Daddy, Benjamin, Lydia—you've got some good friends. And there's yourself. Don't forget him, will you?" *

All your life, you have to stick by your uniqueness. You can't be exactly like anyone else and no one can take over for you. You become a "self" at the price of "taking a stand" for or against something daily. Gradually, you become certain of what you *want* to stand for and against, what you *can* believe in, what you *dare* "hold on to."

However, what rings honest and true for you may not seem "right" to another person wrestling to find values true for him; no one can know what he believes in and stands for until he has lived what he believes. You can't stand up and be counted without knowing whether you believe what people are counting on you for! You can't offer to bet your life on a belief until you can differentiate between values— just as you can't give yourself until you have a "self" to give!

Growth like this cannot be counted in years. Circumstances of life sometimes *force* a teenager into considering "Why is life worth living?" If he can face this basic question and, consciously, choose positive values by which he will live, this person's life has more meaning at adolescence than

* Robert Henriques, *No Arms, No Armour*, Farrar, Straus and Cudahy, Inc., New York, 1940, pp. 199–200 (adapted in part).

does the life of some people seventy years old. Let Anne Frank, a teenager whose remarkable diary was published in 1952, speak. Anne's family fled Germany for Holland when Hitler came to power. When the Nazis occupied Holland, the family went into hiding in a deserted office building in Amsterdam. After two years, the Gestapo discovered them and Anne died in a concentration camp. Who would have more right to be bitter about life? Yet this is what she wrote:

It's hard for us young ones to hold our ground and maintain our opinions in a time when all ideals are being shattered and destroyed, when people are showing their worst side and do not know whether to believe in truth and right and God. Anyone who claims that the older ones have a more difficult time certainly doesn't realize to what extent our problems weigh down on us, problems for which we are probably much too young, but which thrust themselves upon us continually, until, after a long time, we think we've found a solution, but the solution doesn't seem able to resist the facts which reduce it to nothing again. That's the difficulty in these times: ideals, dreams and cherished hopes rise within us, only to meet the horrible truth and be shattered.

It's really a wonder that I haven't dropped all my ideals, because they seem so absurd and impossible to carry out. Yet I keep them, because in spite of everything I still believe that people are really good at heart.—I see the world gradually being turned into a wilderness—I can feel the sufferings of millions and yet, if I look up into the heavens, I think that it will all come right, that this cruelty will end and that peace and tranquility will return again.*

* Anne Frank, *The Diary of a Young Girl*, Doubleday & Company, Inc., New York, 1952, p. 278.

Anne showed no cowardice; she refused to accept evil as final. She chose to believe in life, not death. She could even believe in a better world!

For those teenagers who have had unhappy lives because of illness, accidents, deformities, family quarreling, divorce, drinking, death, drug addiction, or crime—for you also the world has often seemed a wilderness. You have felt alone, as though you, with your personal difficulties, were a separate unit compelled to meet in your own way the problem of being young in a seemingly hopeless world. The "aloneness" of freedom is frightening—while the search for something to hold on to and to live for seems futile!

Like Anne, most teenagers are not cowards. From among the ruins, you've tried to build new hopes. It's been hard work; there is no smooth road to the future, so you scramble over obstacles, or you build around them, but you go on. You don't cling helplessly to someone. You accept independence—or "aloneness"; you know it's no good trying to get rid of it. True, sometimes people ease the aloneness. You gain new courage when you feel someone's love and respect for the battered, beautiful thing any human spirit is. You welcome, as they come, times when you feel close to your family and friends. But they've got to come; you can't force them.

You—and Anne—have refused to become tragic about yourself and your lot in life. You don't blame other people for what you are; you accept responsibility for your own life. You've learned that, regardless of what parents and friends do *to* you and *for* you, you must "walk on" alone with whatever you've built up in yourself as your only guide.

Anne Frank, at fourteen, knew that life is capable of offering beauty and adventure, pain and disappointment, courage, love, work, achievement, freedom and responsibility. If you give all you have and demand the same in return, if you continually strive for ideals such as these, having nothing to do with lesser ones, your life will gain meaning and significance. Nothing else matters—not even death! In the cemetery of the small town of Zermatt, Switzerland, near the magnetically challenging peak of the Matterhorn, are the graves of many young people who lost their lives in attempts to fulfill their dream of beauty and adventure, courage and achievement—to climb the Matterhorn! The inscriptions on their graves are shouts of triumph over death: "To the unwise, they seemed to die."—"Entered the fuller life at dawn from the Matterhorn."

What endures? Your life and your future are so entirely reliant upon others that, without mutual understanding, all of us are dismembered bodies. We cannot run away from one another. Nor are we different from each other, as some people still insist. We are alike: humans yearning toward "humanism," wanderers all in a world shrunk so that faraway places with strange-sounding names are but an atomic-bomb-laden plane's short hop from us! We are cowering children in a world so large and yet so small that the very minuteness is almost too vast to comprehend!

Never before this generation have all nations been swept into a world community of intimate and inescapable relations. Thornton Wilder, a few years ago, wrote that one of the profound changes of this century would be a growing feeling of human kinship, a sense of the oneness of mankind, of multitude, yet of organic unity. Now we understand him. Our mutual danger is the very instrument wearing thin those high and absolute barriers which, in the mind of traditional diplomacy, hedged in a country and cut off its people from others.

To many teenagers, the smallness of the world and the closeness of humanity is a thrilling challenge, not a threat. Not all young people are "being dragged screaming into the twentieth century" of supersonic flight, annihilated distances, and atomic chain reactions. Not all are afraid. Many see that it is not an evil thing, but good, that races and nations shall learn, even by suffering, their interdependence, that we are of each other—sands on the same beach, a poet once wrote, brothers in the same great house of God.

No one can predict the future; but we can look at our present world and predict that, if there is to be a future, man must share and control his machines. Instant communication or transportation by land, sea, and air is available by the lifting of a receiver or the pressing of a button. The world grows smaller day by day. Automation has brought into being machines with uncanny facility in the production of food, shelter, clothing, and a thousand services. Our standard of living has gone to higher levels year by year. At the same time, we face unspeakable instruments of destruction, culminating in a bomb by which, we are told, mankind itself may be destroyed. This means, unmistakably, that we must decide whether we shall live together as human beings in peace or grapple at each other's throats.

Man's survival depends upon his reading significance into his machines—his ships, his planes, his atomic energy. Will he use them for man—or against man? Man was meant to be a rational, moral being, brother to every other man, each a sharer in the world's goods. But some human beings have become the victims of other human beings. In some countries man has become a mere tool, market commodity, or puppet. When man's humanity is rejected, all other values are futile.

As American young people, will you give the world a convincing demonstration of our democratic strength in the exaltation of human life above other values in a changing world? Will you and your children strive on together in this faith, with inward peace as outer tempests rage—strong in the knowledge that man endures forever in a universe of law, struggling upward, however slowly and desperately, by the light of his imperishable dream of freedom and brotherhood? Hate and prejudice, bigotry, fear, and selfish greed —all over the world—are doing their utmost to dispel these ideas. They will not prevail; no man can give or take away values. Hundreds of millions of people are rising to meet the challenge of the enslaver, to cry shame to all forms of human bondage. They will never turn back.

Conditioned by a universe of law, man has gained measurable dominion over it in exact proportion as he has painfully learned and heeded the mandates of *natural* law. Man can learn to face the terrors which surround him by obeying the *eternal* laws of his moral nature: that man is indestructible; he will survive and walk the earth safely.

Every man moves at the center of some hope and struggle and dream; these hopes and dreams of the human race will survive. Though fiery destruction sear from the earth hundreds of millions of people and reduce its cities and monuments to ashes, human life will endure. A man and a woman somewhere will have children. They will learn all over again the enduring values of work, love, cooperation, brotherhood, and worship.

It is not to the outer forms of civilization that we give our last full measure of devotion. Only spiritual realities live on forever; the unalterable meaning of democracy—reverence for the sanctity of every human being; our dream of a time when neither the status nor the service of any man, nor his right to what is his own, shall be determined by race or creed or color, but solely by his human worth in character and competence. This is the dream—that every man shall be equally free to claim the rights with which his Creator has endowed him—the right to life, liberty, and the pursuit of happiness.*

How can one be certain that these values will endure? Because we believe in people, in ongoing life, in youth. Let one of our greatest American poets speak:

> One thing I know deep out of my time: youth when lighted and alive and given a sporting chance is strong for struggle and not afraid of any toils or punishments or dangers or deaths.
>
> What shall be the course of society and civilization across the next hundred years?
>
> For the answers read if you can the strange and baffling eyes of youth.
>
> Yes, for the answers, read, if you can, the strange and baffling eyes of youth.†

* Last six paragraphs adapted in part from Leslie Pinckney Hill, "Enduring Values in a Changing World," Pennsylvania School Journal, vol. XC, no. 6 (February, 1951), pp. 231–232.

† Carl Sandburg, *Always the Young Strangers*, Harcourt, Brace and Company, Inc., New York, 1952, p. 304.